Tiger at the Gates

(LA GUERRE DE TROIE N'AURA PAS LIEU)

JEAN GIRAUDOUX

Tiger at the Gates
(LA GUERRE DE TROIE N'AURA PAS LIEU)

Translated by
CHRISTOPHER FRY

New York
OXFORD UNIVERSITY PRESS

Frontis by Armstrong Jones
Photographs facing pages 24 and 36 by Leo Friedman

PRINTED IN THE UNITED STATES OF AMERICA

3-1303-00046-6962

THE PLAYWRIGHTS' COMPANY (in association with Henry M. Margolis) presented TIGER AT THE GATES in the Robert L. Joseph production on October 3, 1955, at the Plymouth Theatre, New York City, with the following cast:

HECTOR	MICHAEL REDGRAVE
Andromache, *wife to Hector*	Barbara Jefford
Cassandra, *sister to Hector*	Leueen MacGrath
Laundress	Judith Braun
Paris, *brother to Hector*	Leo Ciceri
First Old Man	Howard Caine
Second Old Man	Jack Bittner
Priam, *King of Troy, father to Hector*	Morris Carnovsky
Demekos, *a Poet, Leader of the Senate*	John Laurie
Hecuba, *mother to Hector*	Catherine Lacey
Mathematician	Milton Selzer
Lady in Waiting	Jacqueline Brookes
Polyxene, *young sister to Hector*	Ellen Christopher
Helen	Diane Cilento
Messenger	Ernest Graves
Troilus, *young brother to Hector*	Peter Kerr
Abneos, *a Senator*	Howard Caine
Busiris, *a Lawyer*	Wyndham Goldie
Ajax, *a Greek Captain*	Felix Munso
Ulysses	Walter Fitzgerald
A Topman, *Officer on Paris' Ship*	Nehemiah Persoff
Olpides, *Sailor on Paris' Ship*	Jack Bittner
Senator	Tom McDermott
Sailor	Louis Criss

Directed by Harold Clurman
Designed by Loudon Sainthill
Incidental Music by Lennox Berkeley

ACT I

ACT I

ANDROMACHE. There's not going to be a Trojan War, Cassandra!

CASSANDRA. I shall take that bet, Andromache.

ANDROMACHE. The Greeks are quite right to protest. We are going to receive their ambassador very civilly. We shall wrap up his little Helen and give her back to him.

CASSANDRA. We shall receive him atrociously. We shall refuse to give Helen back. And there *will* be a Trojan War.

ANDROMACHE. Yes, if Hector were not here. But he is here, Cassandra, he is home again. You can hear the trumpets. At this moment he is marching into the city, victorious. And Hector is certainly going to have something to say. When he left, three months ago, he promised me this war would be the last.

CASSANDRA. It is the last. The next is still ahead of him.

ANDROMACHE. Doesn't it ever tire you to see and prophesy only disasters?

CASSANDRA. I see nothing. I prophesy nothing. All I ever do is to take account of two great stupidities: the stupidity of men, and the wild stupidity of the elements.

ANDROMACHE. Why should there be a war? Paris and Helen don't care for each other any longer.

CASSANDRA. Do you think it will matter if Paris and Helen don't care for each other any longer? Has destiny ever been interested in whether things were still true or not?

ANDROMACHE. I don't know what destiny is.

CASSANDRA. I'll tell you. It is simply the relentless logic of each day we live.

ANDROMACHE. I don't understand abstractions.

CASSANDRA. Never mind. We can try a metaphor. Imagine a tiger. You can understand that? It's a nice, easy metaphor. A sleeping tiger.

ANDROMACHE. Let it sleep.

1

CASSANDRA. There's nothing I should like better. But certain cocksure statements have been prodding him out of his sleep. For some considerable time Troy has been full of them.

ANDROMACHE. Full of what?

CASSANDRA. Of cocksure statements, a confident belief that the world, and the supervision of the world, is the province of mankind in general, and Trojan men and women in particular.

ANDROMACHE. I don't follow you.

CASSANDRA. Hector at this very moment is marching into Troy?

ANDROMACHE. Yes. Hector at this very moment has come home to his wife.

CASSANDRA. And Hector's wife is going to have a child?

ANDROMACHE. Yes; I am going to have a child.

CASSANDRA. Don't you call these statements a little over-confident?

ANDROMACHE. Don't frighten me, Cassandra.

(*A* YOUNG LAUNDRESS *goes past with an armful of linen*)

LAUNDRESS. What a beautiful day, miss!

CASSANDRA. Does it seem so, indeed?

LAUNDRESS. It's the most beautiful Spring day Troy has seen this year.

(*Exit*)

CASSANDRA. Even the laundrymaid is confident!

ANDROMACHE. And so she should be, Cassandra. How can you talk of a war on a day like this? Happiness is falling on us out of the sky.

CASSANDRA. Like a blanket of snow.

ANDROMACHE. And beauty, as well. Look at the sunshine. It is finding more mother-of-pearl on the rooftops of Troy than was ever dragged up from the bed of the sea. And do you hear the sound coming up from the fishermen's houses, and the movement of the trees, like the murmuring of sea shells? If ever there were a chance to see men finding a way to live in peace, it is today. To live in peace, in humility. And to be immortal.

CASSANDRA. Yes, I am sure those cripples who have been carried out to lie in their doorways feel how immortal they are.

ANDROMACHE. And to be good. Do you see that horseman, in the advance-guard, leaning from his saddle to stroke a cat on the battlements? Perhaps this is also going to be the first day of true fellowship between men and the animals.

CASSANDRA. You talk too much. Destiny, the tiger, is getting restive, Andromache!

ANDROMACHE. Restive, maybe, in young girls looking for husbands; but not otherwise.

CASSANDRA. You are wrong. Hector has come home in triumph to the wife he adores. The tiger begins to rouse, and opens one eye. The incurables lie out on their benches in the sun and feel immortal. The tiger stretches himself. Today is the chance for peace to enthrone herself over all the world. The tiger licks his lips. And Andromache is going to have a son! And the horsemen have started leaning from their saddles to stroke tom-cats on the battlements! The tiger starts to prowl.

ANDROMACHE. Be quiet!

CASSANDRA. He climbs noiselessly up the palace steps. He pushes open the doors with his snout. And here he is, here he is!

(HECTOR'S *voice:* Andromache!)

ANDROMACHE. You are lying! It is Hector!
CASSANDRA. Whoever said it was not?

(*Enter* HECTOR)

ANDROMACHE. Hector!
HECTOR. Andromache!

(THEY *embrace*)

And good morning to you, too, Cassandra. Ask Paris to come to me, if you will. As soon as he can.

(CASSANDRA *lingers*)

Have you something to tell me?

ANDROMACHE. Don't listen to her! Some catastrophe or other!

HECTOR. Tell me.

CASSANDRA. Your wife is going to have a child.

(*Exit* CASSANDRA)
(HECTOR *takes* ANDROMACHE *in his arms, leads her to a stone bench, and sits beside her. A short pause*)

HECTOR. Will it be a son or a daughter?

ANDROMACHE. Which did you want to create when you called it into life?

HECTOR. A thousand boys. A thousand girls.

ANDROMACHE. Why? Because it would give you a thousand women to hold in your arms? You are going to be disappointed. It will be a son, one single son.

HECTOR. That may very well be. Usually more boys are born than girls at the end of a war.

ANDROMACHE. And before a war? Which, before a war?

HECTOR. Forget wars, Andromache, even this war. It's over. It lost you a father and a brother, but it gave you back a husband.

ANDROMACHE. It has been too kind. It may think better of it presently.

HECTOR. Don't worry. We won't give it the chance. Directly I leave you I shall go into the square, and formally close the Gates of War. They will never open again.

ANDROMACHE. Close them, then. But they will open again.

HECTOR. You can even tell me the day, perhaps?

ANDROMACHE. I can even tell you the day: the day when the cornfields are heavy and golden, when the vines are stooping, ready for harvest, and every house is sheltering a contented couple.

HECTOR. And peace, no doubt, at its very height?

ANDROMACHE. Yes. And my son is strong and glowing with life.

(HECTOR *embraces her*)

HECTOR. Perhaps your son will be a coward. That's one possible safeguard.

ANDROMACHE. He won't be a coward. But perhaps I shall have cut off the index finger of his right hand.

HECTOR. If every mother cut off her son's right-hand index finger, the armies of the world would fight without index fingers. And if they cut off their sons' right legs, the armies would be one-legged. And if they put out their eyes, the armies would be blind, but there would still be armies: blind armies groping to find the fatal place in the enemy's groin, or to get at his throat.

ANDROMACHE. I would rather kill him.

HECTOR. There's a truly maternal solution to war!

ANDROMACHE. Don't laugh. I can still kill him before he is born.

HECTOR. Don't you want to see him at all, not even for a moment? After that, you would think again. Do you mean never to see your son?

ANDROMACHE. It is your son that interests me. Hector, it's because he is yours, because he is you, that I'm so afraid. You don't know how like you he is. Even in this no-man's-land where he is waiting, he already has everything, all those qualities you brought to this life we live together. He has your tenderness, your silences. If you love war, he will love it. Do you love war?

HECTOR. Why ask such a question?

ANDROMACHE. Admit, sometimes you love it.

HECTOR. If a man can love what takes away hope, and happiness, and all those nearest to his heart.

ANDROMACHE. And you know it can be so. Men do love it.

HECTOR. If they let themselves be fooled by that little burst of divinity the gods give them at the moment of attack.

ANDROMACHE. Ah, there, you see! At the moment of attack you feel like a god.

HECTOR. More often not as much as a man. But sometimes, on certain mornings, you get up from the ground feeling lighter, astonished, altered. Your whole body, and the armour on your back, have a different weight, they seem to be made of a different metal. You are invulnerable. A tenderness comes over you, submerging you, a kind of tenderness of battle: you are tender because you are pitiless; what, in fact, the tenderness of the gods must be. You advance towards the enemy slowly, almost absent-mindedly, but lovingly. And you try not to crush a beetle crossing your path. You brush off the mosquito without hurting it. You never at any time had more respect for the life you meet on your way.

ANDROMACHE. And then the enemy comes?

HECTOR. Then the enemy comes, frothing at the mouth. You pity him; you can see him there, behind the swollen veins and the whites of his eyes, the helpless, willing little man of business, the well-meaning husband and son-in-law who likes to grow his own vegetables. You feel a sort of love for him. You love the wart on his cheek and the cast in his eye. You love him. But he comes on; he is insistent. Then you kill him.

ANDROMACHE. And you bend over the wretched corpse as though you are a god; but you are not a god; you can't give back his life again.

HECTOR. You don't wait to bend over him. There are too many more waiting for you, frothing at the mouth and howling hate. Too many more unassuming, law-abiding family men.

ANDROMACHE. Then you kill them.

HECTOR. You kill them. Such is war.

ANDROMACHE. All of them: you kill them all?

HECTOR. This time we killed them all. Quite deliberately. They belonged to an incorrigibly warlike race, the reason why wars go on and multiply in Asia. Only one of them escaped.

ANDROMACHE. In a thousand years time, there the warlike race will be again, descended from that one man. His escape made all that slaughter futile after all. My son is going to love war, just as you do.

HECTOR. I think, now that I've lost my love for it, I hate it.

ANDROMACHE. How do you come to hate what you once worshipped?

HECTOR. You know what it's like when you find out a friend is a liar? Whatever he says, after that, sounds false, however true it may be. And strangely enough, war used to promise me many kinds of virtue: goodness, generosity, and a contempt for anything base and mean. I felt I owed it all my strength and zest for life, even my private happiness, you, Andromache. And until this last campaign there was no enemy I haven't loved.

ANDROMACHE. Very soon you will say you only kill what you love.

HECTOR. It's hard to explain how all the sounds of war combined to make me think it was something noble. The galloping of horse in the night, the clatter of bowls and dishes where the cooks were moving in and out of the firelight, the brush of silk and metal against your tent as the night-patrol went past, and the cry of the falcon wheeling high above the sleeping army and their unsleeping captain: it all seemed then so right, marvellously right.

ANDROMACHE. But not this time: this time war had no music for you?

HECTOR. Why was that? Because I am older? Or was it just the kind of weariness with your job which, for instance, a carpenter will be suddenly seized by, with a table half finished, as I was seized one morning, standing over an adversary of my own age, about to put an end to him? Up to that time, a man I was going to kill had always seemed my direct opposite. This time I was kneeling on a mirror, the death I was going to give was a kind of suicide. I don't know what the carpenter does at such a time, whether he throws away his hammer and plane, or goes on with it.

I went on with it. But after that nothing remained of the perfect trumpet note of war. The spear as it slid against my shield rang suddenly false; so did the shock of the killed against the ground, and, some hours later, the palace crumbling into ruin. And, moreover, war knew that I understood, and gave up any pretence of shame. The cries of the dying sounded false. I had come to that.

ANDROMACHE. But it all still sounded right for the rest of them.

HECTOR. The rest of them heard it as I did. The army I brought back hates war.

ANDROMACHE. An army with poor hearing.

HECTOR. No. When we first came in sight of Troy, an hour ago, you can't imagine how everything in that moment sounded true for them. There wasn't a regiment which didn't halt, racked to the heart by this sense of returning music. So much so, we were afraid to march boldly in through the gates: we broke up into groups outside the walls. It feels like the only job worthy of a good army, laying peaceful siege to the open cities of your own country.

ANDROMACHE. You haven't understood, this is where things are falser than anywhere. War is here, in Troy, Hector. That is what welcomed you at the gates.

HECTOR. What do you mean?

ANDROMACHE. You haven't heard that Paris has carried off Helen?

HECTOR. They told me so. What else?

ANDROMACHE. Did you know that the Greeks are demanding her back? And their ambassador arrives today? And if we don't give her up, it means war.

HECTOR. Why shouldn't we give her up? I shall give her back to them myself.

ANDROMACHE. Paris will never agree to it.

HECTOR. Paris will agree, and very soon. Cassandra is bringing him to me.

ANDROMACHE. But Paris can't agree. His honour, as you all call it, won't let him. Nor his love either, he may tell you.

HECTOR. Well, we shall see. Run and ask Priam if he will let me speak to him at once. And set your heart at rest. All the Trojans who have been fighting, or who can fight, are against a war.

ANDROMACHE. There are still the others, remember.

(*As* ANDROMACHE *goes* . . .
CASSANDRA *enters with* PARIS)

CASSANDRA. Here is Paris.

HECTOR. Congratulations, Paris. I hear you have been very well occupied while we were away.

PARIS. Not badly. Thank you.

HECTOR. What is this story they tell me about Helen?

PARIS. Helen is a very charming person. Isn't she, Cassandra?

CASSANDRA. Fairly charming.

PARIS. Why these reservations today? It was only yesterday you said you thought she was extremely pretty.

CASSANDRA. She is extremely pretty, and fairly charming.

PARIS. Hasn't she the ways of a young, gentle gazelle?

CASSANDRA. No.

PARIS. But you were the one who first said she was like a gazelle.

CASSANDRA. I made a mistake. Since then I have seen a gazelle again.

HECTOR. To hell with gazelles! Doesn't she look any more like a woman than that?

PARIS. She isn't the type of woman we know here, obviously.

CASSANDRA. What is the type of woman we know here?

PARIS. Your type, my dear sister.. The fearfully unremote sort of woman.

CASSANDRA. When your Greek makes love she is a long way off, I suppose?

PARIS. You know perfectly well what I'm trying to say. I have had enough of Asiatic women. They hold you in their arms as though they were glued there, their kisses are like battering-rams, their words chew right into you. The more they undress the more elaborate they seem, until when they're naked they are more overdressed than ever. And they paint their faces to look as though they mean to imprint themselves on you. And they do imprint themselves on you. In short, you are definitely *with* them. But Helen is far away from me, even held in my arms.

HECTOR. Very interesting! But, one wonders, is it really worth a war, to allow Paris to make love at a distance?

CASSANDRA. With distance. He loves women to be distant but right under his nose.

PARIS. To have Helen with you not with you is worth anything in the world.

HECTOR. How did you fetch her away? Willingly, or did you compel her?

PARIS. Listen, Hector! You know women as well as I do. They are only willing when you compel them, but after that they're as enthusiastic as you are.

HECTOR. On horseback, in the usual style of seducers, leaving a heap of horse manure under the windows.

PARIS. Is this a court of enquiry?

HECTOR. Yes, it is. Try for once to answer precisely and accurately. Have you insulted her husband's house, or the Greek earth?

PARIS. The Greek water, a little. She was bathing.

CASSANDRA. She is born of the foam, is she? This cold one is born of the foam, like Venus.

HECTOR. You haven't disfigured the walls of the palace with offensive drawings, as you usually do? You didn't shout to the echoes any word which they would at once repeat to the betrayed husband?

PARIS. No. Menelaus was naked on the river bank, busy removing a crab from his big toe. He watched my boat sail past as if the wind were carrying his clothes away.

HECTOR. Looking furious?

PARIS. The face of a king being nipped by a crab isn't likely to look beatific.

HECTOR. No onlookers?

PARIS. My crew.

HECTOR. Perfect!

PARIS. Why perfect? What are you getting at?

HECTOR. I say perfect, because you have done nothing irre-
vocable. In other words: she was undressed, so neither her
clothes nor her belongings have been insulted. Nothing
except her body, which is negligible. I've enough acquaintance with the Greeks to know they will concoct a divine
adventure out of it, to their own glory, the story of this little
Greek queen who goes down into the sea, and quietly comes
up again a few months later, with a look on her face of
perfect innocence.

CASSANDRA. We can be quite sure of the look on her face.

PARIS. You think that I'm going to take Helen back to
Menelaus?

HECTOR. We don't ask so much of you, or of her. The Greek
ambassador will take care of it. He will put her back in the
sea himself, like a gardener planting water-lilies, at a particular chosen spot. You will give her into his hands this
evening.

PARIS. I don't know whether you are allowing yourself to
notice how monstrous you are being, to suppose that a man
who has the prospect of a night with Helen will agree to
giving it up.

CASSANDRA. You still have an afternoon with Helen. Surely
that's more Greek?

HECTOR. Don't be obstinate. We know you of old. This isn't
the first separation you've accepted.

PARIS. My dear Hector, that's true enough. Up to now I have
always accepted separations fairly cheerfully. Parting from
a woman, however well you love her, induces a most pleasant
state of mind, which I know how to value as well as anybody.
You come out of her arms and take your first lonely walk
through the town, and, the first little dressmaker you meet,
you notice with a shock of surprise how fresh and uncon-
cerned she looks, after that last sight you have had of the
dear face you parted from, her nose red with weeping.
Because you have come away from such broken, despairing

farewells, the laundrygirls and the fruitsellers laughing their heads off, more than make up for whatever you've lost in the parting. By losing one person your life has become entirely re-peopled. All the women in the world have been created for you afresh; they are all your own, in the liberty, honour, and peace of your conscience. Yes, you're quite right: when a love-affair is broken off it reaches its highest point of exaltation. Which is why I shall never be parted from Helen, because with Helen I feel as though I had broken with every other woman in the world, and that gives me the sensation of being free a thousand times over instead of once.

HECTOR. Because she doesn't love you. Everything you say proves it.

PARIS. If you like. But, if I had to choose one out of all the possible ways of passion, I would choose the way Helen doesn't love me.

HECTOR. I'm extremely sorry. But you will give her up.

PARIS. You are not the master here.

HECTOR. I am your elder brother, and the future master.

PARIS. Then order me about in the future. For the present, I obey my father.

HECTOR. That's all I want! You're willing that we should put this to Priam and accept his judgment?

PARIS. Perfectly willing.

HECTOR. On your solemn word? We both swear to accept that?

CASSANDRA. Mind what you're doing, Hector! Priam is mad for Helen. He would rather give up his daughters.

HECTOR. What nonsense is this?

PARIS. For once she is telling the truth about the present instead of the future.

CASSANDRA. And all our brothers, and all our uncles, and all our great-great uncles! Helen has a guard-of-honour which includes every old man in the city. Look there. It is time for her walk. Do you see, there's a fringe of white beards draped all along the battlements?

HECTOR. A beautiful sight. The beards are white, and the faces red.

CASSANDRA. Yes; it's the blood pressure. They should be waiting at the Scamander Gate, to welcome the victorious troops. But no; they are all at the Sceean Gate, waiting for Helen.

HECTOR. Look at them, all leaning forward as one man, like storks when they see a rat going by.

CASSANDRA. The rat is Helen.

PARIS. Is it?

CASSANDRA. There she is: on the second terrace, standing to adjust her sandal, and giving careful thought to the crossing of her legs.

HECTOR. Incredible. All the old men of Troy are there looking down at her.

CASSANDRA. Not all. There are certain crafty ones looking up at her.

(*Cries offstage:* Long live Beauty!)

HECTOR. What are they shouting?

PARIS. They're shouting 'Long live Beauty!'

CASSANDRA. I quite agree with them, if they mean that they themselves should die as quickly as possible.

(*Cries offstage:* Long live Venus!)

HECTOR. And what now?

CASSANDRA. 'Long live Venus.' They are shouting only words without R's in them because of their lack of teeth. Long live Beauty, long live Venus, long live Helen. At least they imagine they're shouting, though, as you can hear, all they are doing is simply increasing a mumble to its highest power.

HECTOR. What has Venus to do with it?

CASSANDRA. They imagine it was Venus who gave us Helen. To show her gratitude to Paris for awarding her the apple on first sight.

HECTOR. That was another brilliant stroke of yours.

PARIS. Stop playing the elder brother!

(*Enter* TWO OLD MEN)

1st OLD MAN. Down there we see her better.

2nd OLD MAN. We had a very good view.

1st OLD MAN. But she can hear us better from up here. Come on. One, two, three!

BOTH. Long live Helen!

2nd OLD MAN. It's a little tiring, at our age, to have to climb up and down these impossible steps all the time, according to whether we want to look at her or to cheer her.

1st OLD MAN. Would you like us to alternate? One day we will cheer her? Another day we will look at her?

2nd OLD MAN. You are mad! One day without looking at Helen, indeed! Goodness me, think what we've seen of her today! One, two, three!

BOTH. Long live Helen!

1st OLD MAN. And now down we go again!

(THEY *run off*)

CASSANDRA. You see what they're like, Hector. I don't know how their poor lungs are going to stand it.

HECTOR. But our father can't be like this.

PARIS. Hector, before we have this out in front of my father, I suppose you wouldn't like to take just one look at Helen.

HECTOR. I don't care a fig about Helen. Ah: greetings to you, father!

(PRIAM *enters, with* HECUBA, ANDROMACHE, *the poet* DEMOKOS *and another old man.* HECUBA *leads by the hand little* POLYXENE)

PRIAM. What was it you said?

HECTOR. I said that we should make haste to shut the Gates of War, father, see them bolted and padlocked, so that not even a gnat can get between them.

PRIAM. I thought what you said was somewhat shorter.

DEMOKOS. He said he didn't care a fig about Helen.

PRIAM. Look over here.

(HECTOR *obeys*)

Do you see her?

HECUBA. Indeed he sees her. Who, I ask myself, doesn't see her, or hasn't seen her? She takes the road which goes the whole way round the city.

DEMOKOS. It is Beauty's perfect circle.

PRIAM. Do you see her?

HECTOR. Yes, I see her. What of it?

DEMOKOS. Priam is asking you what you see.

HECTOR. I see a young woman adjusting her sandal.

CASSANDRA. She takes some time to adjust her sandal.

PARIS. I carried her off naked; she left her clothes in Greece. Those are your sandals, Cassandra. They're a bit big for her.

CASSANDRA. Anything's too big for these little women.

HECTOR. I see two charming buttocks.

HECUBA. He sees what all of you see.

PRIAM. I'm sorry for you!

HECTOR. Why?

PRIAM. I had no idea that the young men of Troy had come to this.

HECTOR. What have they come to?

PRIAM. To being impervious to beauty.

DEMOKOS. And, consequently, ignorant of love. And, consequently, unrealistic. To us who are poets reality is love or nothing.

HECTOR. But the old men, you think, can appreciate love and beauty?

HECUBA. But of course. If you make love, or if you are beautiful, you don't need to understand these things.

HECTOR. You come across beauty, father, at every street corner. I'm not alluding to Helen, though at the moment she condescends to walk our streets.

PRIAM. You are being unfair, Hector. Surely there have been occasions in your life when a woman has seemed to be more than merely herself, as though a radiance of thoughts and

feelings glowed from her flesh, taking a special brilliance
from it.

DEMOKOS. As a ruby represents blood.

HECTOR. Not to those who have seen blood. I have just come
back from a close acquaintance with it.

DEMOKOS. A symbol, you understand. Soldier though you
are, you have surely heard of symbolism! Surely you have
come across women who as soon as you saw them seemed
to you to personify intelligence, harmony, gentleness, whatever it might be?

HECTOR. It has happened.

DEMOKOS. And what did you do?

HECTOR. I went closer, and that was the end of it. And what
does this we see here personify?

DEMOKOS. We have told you before: Beauty.

HECUBA. Then send her quickly back to the Greeks if you
want her to personify that for long. Blonde beauty doesn't
usually last for ever.

DEMOKOS. It's impossible to talk to these women!

HECUBA. Then don't talk *about* women. You're not showing
much gallantry, I might say; nor patriotism either. All other
races choose one of their own women as their symbol, even
if they have flat noses and lips like two fishes on a plate. It's
only you who have to go outside your own country to find it.

HECTOR. Listen, father: we are just back from a war, and we
have come home exhausted. We have made quite certain of
peace on our continent for ever. From now on we mean to
live in happiness, and we mean our wives to be able to love
us without anxiety, and to bear our children.

DEMOKOS. Wise principles, but war has never prevented wives
from having children.

HECTOR. So explain to me why we have come back to find the
city transformed, all because of Helen? Explain to me what
you think she has given to us, worth a quarrel with the
Greeks?

MATHEMATICIAN. Anybody will tell you! I can tell you
myself!

HECUBA. Listen to the mathematician!

MATHEMATICIAN. Yes, listen to the mathematician! And don't think that mathematicians have no concern with women! We're the land-surveyors of your personal landscape. I can't tell you how we mathematicians suffer to see any slight disproportion of the flesh, on the chin or the thigh, any infringement of your geometrical desirability. Well now, until this day mathematicians have never been satisfied with the countryside surrounding Troy. The line linking the plain with the hills seemed to us too slack: the line from the hills to the mountains too taut. Now, since Helen came, the country has taken on meaning and vigour. And, what is particularly evident to true mathematicians, space and volume have now found in Helen a common denominator. We can abolish all the instruments we have invented to reduce the universe to a manageable equation. There are no more feet and inches, ounces, pounds, milligrams or leagues. There is only the weight of Helen's footfall, the length of Helen's arm, the range of Helen's look or voice; and the movement of the air as she goes past is the measure of the winds. That is what the mathematicians will tell you.

HECUBA. The old fool is crying.

PRIAM. My dear son, you have only to look at this crowd, and you will understand what Helen is. She is a kind of absolution. To each one of these old men, whom you can see now like a frieze of grotesque heads all round the city walls: to the old swindler, the old thief, the old pandar, to all the old failures, she has shown they always had a secret longing to rediscover the beauty they had lost. If throughout their lives beauty had always been as close at hand as Helen is today, they would never have tricked their friends, or sold their daughters, or drunk away their inheritance. Helen is like a pardon to them: a new beginning for them, their whole future.

HECTOR. These old men's ancient futures are no concern of mine.

DEMOKOS. Hector, as a poet I approach things by the way of

poetry. Imagine if beauty, never, at any time, touched our language. Imagine there being no such word as 'delight'.

HECTOR. We should get on well enough without it. I get on without it already. 'Delight' is a word I use only when I'm absolutely driven to it.

DEMOKOS. Well, then the word 'desirable': you could get on without that as well, I suppose?

HECTOR. If it could be bought only at the cost of war, yes, I could get on without the word 'desirable'.

DEMOKOS. One of the most beautiful words there are was found only at the cost of war: the word 'courage'.

HECTOR. It has been well paid for.

HECUBA. And the word 'cowardice' was inevitably found at the same time.

PRIAM. My son, why do you so deliberately not understand us?

HECTOR. I understand you very well. With the help of a quibble, by pretending to persuade us to fight for beauty you want to get us to fight for a woman.

PRIAM. Would you never go to war for any woman?

HECTOR. Certainly not!

HECUBA. And he would be unchivalrously right.

CASSANDRA. If there were only one woman, then perhaps he would go to war for her. But we have exceeded that number, quite extravagantly.

DEMOKOS. Wouldn't you go to war to rescue Andromache?

HECTOR. Andromache and I have already made our secret plans for escaping from any prison in the world, and finding our way back to each other again.

DEMOKOS. Even if there's no hope of it on earth?

HECTOR. Even then.

HECUBA. You have done well to unmask them, Hector. They want you to make war for the sake of a woman; it's the kind of lovemaking men believe in who are past making love in any other way.

DEMOKOS. And doesn't that make you all the more valuable?

HECUBA. Ah yes! You may say so!

DEMOKOS. Excuse me, but I can't agree with you. The sex which gave me my mother will always have my respect, even its least worthy representatives.

HECUBA. We know that. You have, as we know, shown your respect for instance to ——

(*The* SERVANTS *who have stood by to hear the argument burst out laughing*)

PRIAM. Hecuba! Daughters! What can this mean? Why on earth are you all so up in arms? The Council are considering giving the city a public holiday in honour of one of your sex.

ANDROMACHE. I know of only one humiliation for a woman: injustice.

DEMOKOS. It's painful to say so, but there's no one knows less what a woman is than a woman.

(*The* YOUNG SERVANT, *passing:* Oh, dear! dear!)

HECUBA. We know perfectly well. I will tell you myself what a woman is.

DEMOKOS. Don't let them talk, Priam. You never know what they might say.

HECUBA. They might tell the truth.

PRIAM. I have only to think of one of you, my dears, to know what a woman is.

DEMOKOS. In the first place, she is the source of our energy. You know that, Hector. The soldiers who haven't a portrait of a woman in their kit aren't worth anything.

CASSANDRA. The source of your pride, yes, I agree.

HECUBA. Of your vices.

ANDROMACHE. She is a poor bundle of uncertainty, a poor mass of fears, who detests whatever is difficult, and adores whatever is vulgar and easy.

HECTOR. Dear Andromache!

HECUBA. It's very simple. I have been a woman for fifty years, and I've never yet been able to discover precisely what it is I am.

DEMOKOS. Secondly, whether she likes it or not, she's the only reward for courage. Ask any soldier. To kill a man is to merit a woman.

ANDROMACHE. She loves cowards and libertines. If Hector were a coward or a libertine I shouldn't love him less; I might even love him more.

PRIAM. Don't go too far, Andromache. You will prove the very opposite of what you want to prove.

POLYXENE. She is greedy. She tells lies.

DEMOKOS. So we're to say nothing of her fidelity, her purity: we are not to mention them?

THE SERVANT. Oh, dear! dear!

DEMOKOS. What did you say?

THE SERVANT. I said 'Oh, dear! dear!' I say what I think.

POLYXENE. She breaks her toys. She puts them headfirst into boiling water.

HECUBA. The older we women grow, the more clearly we see what men really are: hypocrites, boasters, he-goats. The older men grow, the more they doll us up with every perfection. There isn't a slut you've hugged behind a wall who isn't transformed in your memories into a loved and lovely creature.

PRIAM. Have you ever deceived me, Hecuba?

HECUBA. Only with yourself; scores of time with yourself.

DEMOKOS. Has Andromache ever deceived Hector?

HECUBA. You can leave Andromache out of this. There is nothing she could recognize in the sad histories of erring women.

ANDROMACHE. But I know if Hector were not my husband, if he were a club-footed, bandy-legged fisherman I should run after him and find him in his hovel, and lie down on the pile of oyster-shells and seaweed, and give him a son in adultery.

POLYXENE. She pretends to go to sleep at night, but she's really playing games in her head with her eyes shut.

HECUBA (*to* POLYXENE). You may well say so! It's dreadful! You know how I scold you for it!

THE SERVANT. The only thing worse than a woman is a man; there are no words to describe him.

DEMOKOS. Then more's the pity if a woman deceives us! More's the pity if she scorns her own value and dignity! If she can't be true to a pattern of perfection which would save her from the ravages of conscience, we have to do it for her.

THE SERVANT. Oh, the kind guardian angel!

PARIS. One thing they've forgotten to say of themselves: they are never jealous.

PRIAM. My dear daughters, the fact that you're so furious is a proof in itself that we are right. I can't conceive of any greater unselfishness than the way you now fight for peace, when peace will give you idle, feeble, chicken-hearted husbands, and war would turn them into men.

DEMOKOS. Into heroes.

HECUBA. Yes, we know the jargon. In war-time a man is called a hero. It doesn't make him any braver, and he runs for his life. But at least it's a hero who is running away.

ANDROMACHE. Father, I must beg you to listen. If you have such a fondness for women, listen to what they have to say to you, for I can promise I speak for all the women in the world. Let us keep our husbands as they are. The gods took care to see they were surrounded with enough obstacles and dangers to keep them brave and vigorous. Quite enough if they had nothing to cope with except floods and storms! Or only wild animals! The small game, foxes and hares and pheasants, which a woman can scarcely distinguish from the heather they hide in, prove a man's quickness of eye far better than this target you propose: the enemy's heart hiding in flesh and metal. Whenever I have seen a man kill a stag or an eagle, I have offered up thanks to them. I know they died for Hector. Why should you want me to owe Hector to the deaths of other men?

PRIAM. I don't want it, my dear child. But why do you think you are here now, all looking so beautiful, and valiantly demanding peace? Why: because your husbands and your fathers, and their fathers, and theirs, were fighting men. If they had been too lazy and self-indulgent to spring to arms, if they hadn't known how this dull and stupid business we call life suddenly leaps into flame and justifies itself through the scorn men have for it, you would find *you* were the cowards now, and you would be clamouring for war. A man has only one way of being immortal on this earth: he has to forget he is mortal.

ANDROMACHE. Why, exactly so, father: you're only too right. The brave men die in war. It takes great luck or judgment not to be killed. Once at least the head has to bow and the knee has to bend to danger. The soldiers who march back under the triumphal arches are death's deserters. How can a country increase in strength and honour by sending them both to their graves?

PRIAM. Daughter, the first sign of cowardice in a people is their first moment of decay.

ANDROMACHE. But which is the worse cowardice? To appear cowardly to others, and make sure of peace? Or to be cowardly in your own eyes, and let loose a war?

DEMOKOS. Cowardice is not to prefer death on every hand rather than the death of one's native land.

HECUBA. I was expecting poetry at this point. It never lets us down.

ANDROMACHE. Everyone always dies for his country. If you have lived in it, well and wisely and actively, you die for it too.

HECUBA. It would be better if only the old men fought the wars. Every country is the country of youth. When its youth dies it dies with them.

DEMOKOS. All this nonsense about youth! In thirty years time youth is nothing but these old men you talk about.

CASSANDRA. Wrong.

HECUBA. Wrong! When a grown man reaches forty we change him for an old one. He has completely disappeared. There's only the most superficial resemblance between the two of them. Nothing is handed on from one to the other.

DEMOKOS. I still take a serious concern in my fame as a poet.

HECUBA. Yes, that's quite true. And your rheumatism.

(*Another outburst of laughter from the* SERVANTS)

HECTOR. And you can listen to all this without saying a word, Paris? Can you still not decide to give up an adventure to save us from years of unhappiness and massacre?

PARIS. What do you want me to say? My case is an international problem.

HECTOR. Are you really in love with Helen, Paris?

CASSANDRA. They've become now a kind of symbol of love's devotion. They don't still have to love each other.

PARIS. I worship Helen.

CASSANDRA (*at the rampart*). Here she is.

HECTOR. If I persuade her to set sail, will you agree?

PARIS. Yes, I'll agree.

HECTOR. Father, if Helen is willing to go back to Greece, will you hold her here by force?

PRIAM. Why discuss the impossible?

HECTOR. Do you call it impossible? If women are a tenth of what you say they are, Helen will go of her own free will.

PARIS. Father, now *I'm* going to ask you to let him do what he wants. You have seen what it's like. As soon as the question of Helen cropped up, this whole tribe royal turned itself into a family conclave of all the poor girl's sisters-in-law, mother- and father-in-law, brother-in-law, worthy of the best middle-class tradition. I doubt if there's anything more humiliating than to be cast for the part of the seducer son in a large family. I've had quite enough of their insinuations. I accept Hector's challenge.

DEMOKOS. Helen's not only yours, Paris. She belongs to the city. She belongs to our country.

MATHEMATICIAN. She belongs to the landscape.

HECUBA. You be quiet, mathematician.

CASSANDRA. Here's Helen; here she is.

HECTOR. Father, I must ask you to let me handle this. Listen; they are calling us to go to the ceremony, to close the Gates of War. Leave this to me. I'll join you soon.

PRIAM. Do you really agree to this, Paris?

PARIS. I'm eager for it.

PRIAM. Very well, then; let it be so. Come along, the rest of you; we will see that the Gates of War are made ready.

CASSANDRA. Those poor gates. They need more oil to shut them than to open them.

> (PARIS *and the rest withdraw.*
> DEMOKOS *stays*)

HECTOR. What are you waiting for?

DEMOKOS. The visitation of my genius.

HECTOR. Say that again?

DEMOKOS. Every time Helen walks my way I am thrown into a transport of inspiration. I shake all over, break into sweat, and improvise. Good heavens, here it is! (*He declaims:*)
> Beautiful Helen, Helen of Sparta,
>> Singular as the evening star,
> The gods forbid that we should part a
> Pair as fair as you and Paris are.

HECTOR. Your line-endings give me a headache.

DEMOKOS. It's an invention of mine. I can obtain effects even more surprising. Listen: (*declaims*)
> Face the great Hector with no qualm,
>> Troy's glory though he be, and the
>> world's terror:
> He is the storm, and you the after-calm,
>> Yours is the right, and his the boist'rous
>> error.

HECTOR. Get out!

DEMOKOS. What are you glaring at? You look as though you have as little liking for poetry as you have for war.

HECTOR. They make a pretty couple! Now vanish.

> (*Exit* DEMOKOS)
> (*Enter* CASSANDRA)

CASSANDRA. Helen!

> (*Enter* HELEN *and* PARIS)

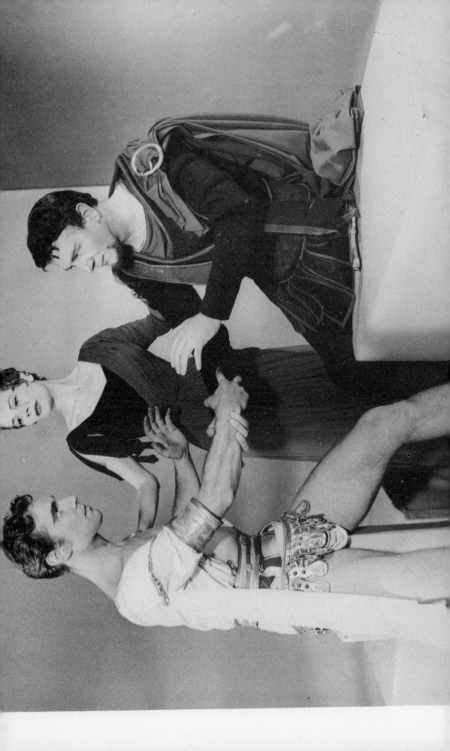

PARIS. Here he is, Helen darling; this is Hector. He has a
proposition to make to you, a perfectly simple proposition.
He wants to hand you over to the Greeks, and prove to you
that you don't love me. Tell me you do love me, before I
leave you with him. Tell me in your own words.

HELEN. I adore you, my sweet.

PARIS. Tell me how beautiful the wave was which swept you
away from Greece.

HELEN. Magnificent! A magnificent wave! Where did you see
a wave? The sea was so calm.

PARIS. Tell me you hate Menelaus.

HELEN. Menelaus? I hate him.

PARIS. You haven't finished yet. I shall never again return to
Greece. Say that.

HELEN. You will never again return to Greece.

PARIS. No, no, this is about you, my darling.

HELEN. Oh, of course! How silly I am! I shall never again
return to Greece.

PARIS. I didn't make her say it. – Now it's up to you.

(HE *goes off*)

HECTOR. Is Greece a beautiful country?

HELEN. Paris found it ravishing.

HECTOR. I meant is Greece itself beautiful, apart from Helen?

HELEN. How very charming of you.

HECTOR. I was simply wondering what it is really like.

HELEN. Well, there are quite a great many kings, and a great
many goats, dotted about on marble.

HECTOR. If the kings are in gold, and the goats angora, that
would look pretty well when the sun was rising.

HELEN. I don't get up very early.

HECTOR. And a great many gods as well, I believe? Paris
tells me the sky is crawling with them; he tells me you can
see the legs of goddesses hanging down from the clouds.

HELEN. Paris always goes about with his nose in the air. He
may have seen them.

HECTOR. But you haven't?

HELEN. I am not gifted that way. I will look out for them when I go back there again.

HECTOR. You were telling Paris you would never be going back there.

HELEN. He asked me to tell him so. I adore doing what Paris wants me to do.

HECTOR. I see. Is that also true of what you said about Menelaus? Do you not, after all, hate him?

HELEN. Why should I hate him?

HECTOR. For the one reason which might certainly make for hate. You have seen too much of him.

HELEN. Menelaus? Oh, no! I have never seen Menelaus. On the contrary.

HECTOR. You have never seen your husband?

HELEN. There are some things, and certain people, that stand out in bright colours for me. They are the ones I can see. I believe in them. I have never been able to see Menelaus.

HECTOR. Though I suppose he must have come very close to you sometimes.

HELEN. I have been able to touch him. But I can't honestly tell you I saw him.

HECTOR. They say he never left your side.

HELEN. Apparently. I must have walked across him a great many times without knowing it.

HECTOR. Whereas you have seen Paris.

HELEN. Vividly; in the clearest outline against the sky and the sun.

HECTOR. Does he still stand out as vividly as he did? Look down there: leaning against the rampart.

HELEN. Are you sure that's Paris, down there?

HECTOR. He is waiting for you.

HELEN. Good gracious! He's not nearly as clear as usual!

HECTOR. And yet the wall is freshly whitewashed. Look again: there he is in profile.

HELEN. It's odd how people waiting for you stand out far less clearly than people you are waiting for.

HECTOR. Are you sure that Paris loves you?

HELEN. I don't like knowing about other people's feelings. There is nothing more embarrassing. Just as when you play cards and you see your opponent's hand. You are sure to lose.

HECTOR. What about yourself? Do you love him?

HELEN. I don't much like knowing my own feelings either.

HECTOR. But, listen: when you make love with Paris, when he sleeps in your arms, when you are circled round with Paris, overwhelmed with Paris, haven't you any thoughts about it?

HELEN. My part is over. I leave any thinking to the universe. It does it much better than I do.

HECTOR. Have there been many others, before Paris?

HELEN. Some.

HECTOR. And there will be others after him, wouldn't you say, as long as they stand out in clear relief against the sky, or the wall, or the white sheets on the bed? It is just as I thought it was. You don't love Paris particularly, Helen; you love men.

HELEN. I don't dislike them. They're as pleasant as soap and a sponge and warm water; you feel cleansed and refreshed by them.

HECTOR. Cassandra! Cassandra!

CASSANDRA (*entering*). What do you want?

HECTOR. Cassandra, Helen is going back this evening with the Greek ambassador.

HELEN. I? What makes you think so?

HECTOR. Weren't you telling me that you didn't love Paris particularly?

HELEN. That was your interpretation. Still, if you like.

HECTOR. I quote my authority. You have the same liking for men as you have for a cake of soap.

HELEN. Yes; or pumice stone perhaps is better. What about it?

HECTOR. Well, then, you're not going to hesitate in your choice between going back to Greece, which you don't mind, and a catastrophe as terrible as war?

HELEN You don't understand me at all, Hector. Of course
I'm not hesitating. It would be very easy to say 'I will do
this or that, so that this can happen or that can happen'.
You've discovered my weakness and you are overjoyed. The
man who discovers a woman's weakness is like the huntsman
in the heat of the day who finds a cool spring. He wallows in
it. But you mustn't think, because you have convinced me,
you've convinced the future, too. Merely by making children
behave as you want them to, you don't alter the course of
destiny.

HECTOR. I don't follow your Greek shades and subtleties.

HELEN. It's not a question of shades and subtleties. It's no less
than a question of monsters and pyramids.

HECTOR. Do you choose to leave here, yes or no?

HELEN. Don't bully me. I choose what happens in the way I
choose men, or anything else. I choose whatever is not
indefinite and vague. I choose what I see.

HECTOR. I know, you said that: what you see in the brightest
colours. And you don't see yourself returning to Menelaus
in a few days' time?

HELEN. No. It's very difficult.

HECTOR. We could no doubt persuade your husband to dress
with great brilliance for your return.

HELEN. All the purple dye from all the murex shells in the sea
wouldn't make him visible to me.

HECTOR. Here you have a rival, Cassandra. Helen can read
the future, too.

HELEN. No, I can't read the future. But when I imagine the
future some of the pictures I see are coloured, and some are
dull and drab. And up to now it has always been the coloured
scenes which have happened in the end.

HECTOR. We are going to give you back to the Greeks at high
noon, on the blinding sand, between the violet sea and the
ochre-coloured wall. We shall all be in golden armour with
red skirts; and my sisters, dressed in green and standing
between my white stallion and Priam's black mare, will
return you to the Greek ambassador, over whose silver

helmet I can imagine tall purple plumes. You see that, I think?

HELEN. No, none of it. It is all quite sombre.

HECTOR. You are mocking me, aren't you?

HELEN. Why should I mock you? Very well, then. Let us go, if you like! Let us go and get ready to return me to the Greeks. We shall see what happens.

HECTOR. Do you realize how you insult humanity, or is it unconscious?

HELEN. I don't know what you mean.

HECTOR. You realize that your coloured picture-book is holding the world up to ridicule? While we are all battling and making sacrifices to bring about a time we can call our own, there are you, looking at your pictures which nothing in all eternity can alter. What's wrong? Which one has made you stop and stare at it with those blind eyes? I don't doubt it's the one where you are standing here on the ramparts, watching the battle going on below. Is it the battle you see?

HELEN. Yes.

HECTOR. And the city is in ruins or burning, isn't that so?

HELEN. Yes. It's a vivid red.

HECTOR. And what about Paris? You are seeing his body dragged behind a chariot?

HELEN. Oh, do you think that is Paris? I see what looks like a flash of sunlight rolling in the dust. A diamond sparkling on his hand. Yes, it is! Often I don't recognize faces, but I always recognize the jewellery. It's his ring, I'm quite certain.

HECTOR. Exactly. Do I dare to ask you about Andromache, and myself, the scene of Andromache and Hector? You are looking at us. Don't deny it. How do you see us? Happy, grown old, bathed in light?

HELEN. I am not trying to see it.

HECTOR. The scene of Andromache weeping over the body of Hector, does that shine clearer?

HELEN. You seem to know. But sometimes I see things shining, brilliantly shining, and they never happen. No one is infallible.

HECTOR. You needn't go on. I understand. There is a son between the weeping mother and the father stretched on the ground?

HELEN. Yes. He is playing with his father's tangled hair. He is a sweet boy.

HECTOR. And these scenes are there in your eyes, down in the depths of them. Could I see them there?

HELEN. I don't know. Look.

HECTOR. Nothing. Nothing except the ashes of all those fires, the gold and the emerald in dust. How innocent it is, this crystal where the future is waiting. But there should be tears bathing it, and where are they? Would you cry, Helen, if you were going to be killed?

HELEN. I don't know. But I should scream. And I feel I shall scream if you go on at me like this, Hector. I am going to scream.

HECTOR. You will leave for Greece this evening, Helen, otherwise I shall kill you.

HELEN. But I want to leave! I'm prepared to leave. All that I'm trying to tell is that I simply can't manage to distinguish the ship that is going to carry me there. Nothing is shining in the least, neither the metal on the mast, nor the ring in the captain's nose, nor the cabin-boy's eyes, nor anything.

HECTOR. You will go back on a grey sea under a grey sun. But we must have peace.

HELEN. I cannot see peace.

HECTOR. Ask Cassandra to make her appear for you. Cassandra is a sorceress. She can summon up shapes and spirits.

A MESSENGER (*entering*). Hector, Priam is asking for you. The priests are opposed to our shutting the Gates of War. They say the gods will consider it an insult.

HECTOR. It is curious how the gods can never speak for themselves in these difficult matters.

MESSENGER. They have spoken for themselves. A thunderbolt has fallen on the temple, several men have been killed, the entrails of the victims have been consulted, and they are unanimously against Helen's return to Greece.

HECTOR. I would give a good deal to be able to consult the entrails of the priests . . . I'll follow you.

(*The* MESSENGER *goes*)

Well, now, Helen, do we agree about this?

HELEN. Yes.

HECTOR. From now on you will say what I tell you to say? You will do what I tell you to do?

HELEN. Yes.

HECTOR. When we come in front of Ulysses you won't contradict me, you will bear out everything I say?

HELEN. Yes.

HECTOR. Do you hear this, Cassandra? Listen to this solid wall of negation which says Yes! They have all given in to me. Paris has given in to me, Priam has given in to me, Helen has given in to me. And yet I can't help feeling that in each of these apparent victories I have been defeated. You set out, thinking you are going to have to wrestle with giants; you brace yourself to conquer them, and you find yourself wrestling with something inflexible reflected in a woman's eye. You have said yes beautifully, Helen, and you're brimful of a stubborn determination to defy me!

HELEN. That's possible. But how can I help it? It isn't my own determination.

HECTOR. By what peculiar vagary did the world choose to place its mirror in this obtuse head?

HELEN. It's most regrettable, obviously. But can you see any way of defeating the obstinacy of a mirror?

HECTOR. Yes. I've been considering that for the past several minutes.

ANOTHER MESSENGER (*entering*). Hector, make haste. They are in a turmoil of revolt down on the beach. The Greek ships have been sighted, and they have hoisted their flag not masthead but hatchway. The honour of our navy is at stake.

Priam is afraid the ambassador may be murdered as soon as
he lands.

HECTOR. I leave you in charge of Helen, Cassandra. I must
go and give my orders.

HELEN. If you break the mirror, will what is reflected in it
cease to exist?

HECTOR. That is the whole question.

(*Exit* HECTOR)

CASSANDRA. I never see anything at all, you know, either
coloured or not. But I can feel the weight on me of every
person who comes towards me. I know what is in store for
them by the sensation of suffering which flows into my veins.

HELEN. Is it true that you are a sorceress? Could you really
make Peace take shape and appear for us?

CASSANDRA. Peace? Very easily. She is always standing in
her beggarly way on every threshold. Wait . . . you will see
her now.

(PEACE *appears*)

HELEN. Oh, how pretty she is!

PEACE. Come to my rescue, Helen: help me!

HELEN. But how pale and wan she is.

PEACE. Pale and wan? What do you mean? Don't you see
the gold shining in my hair?

HELEN. Gold? Well, perhaps a golden grey. It's very original.

PEACE. Golden grey? Is my gold now grey?

(SHE *disappears*)

CASSANDRA. I think she means to make herself clearer.

(PEACE *re-appears, outrageously painted*)

PEACE. Is that better now?

HELEN. I don't see her as well as I did before.

PEACE. Is that better?

CASSANDRA. Helen doesn't see you as well as she did.

PEACE. But you can see me: you are speaking to me.

CASSANDRA. It's my speciality to speak to the invisible.

PEACE. What is going on, then? Why are all the men in the city and along the beach making such a pandemonium?

CASSANDRA. Apparently their gods are insulted, and their honour is at stake.

PEACE. Their gods! Their honour!

CASSANDRA. Yes . . . You are ill!

THE CURTAIN FALLS

ACT II

ACT II

A palace enclosure. At each corner a view of the sea. In the middle a monument, the Gates of War. They are wide open.

(HELEN. *The young* TROILUS)

HELEN. You, you, hey! You down there! Yes, it's you I'm calling. Come here.

TROILUS. No.

HELEN. What is your name?

TROILUS. Troilus.

HELEN. Come here.

TROILUS. No.

HELEN. Come here, Troilus!

(TROILUS *draws near*)

That's the way. You obey when you're called by your name: you are still very like a puppy. It's rather beguiling. Do you know you have made me call out to a man for the first time in my life. They keep so close to my side I have only usually to move my lips. I have called out to sea-gulls, to dogs, to the echoes, but never before to a man. You will pay for that. What's the matter? Are you trembling?

TROILUS. No, I'm not.

HELEN. You tremble, Troilus.

TROILUS. Yes, I do.

HELEN. Why are you always just behind me? If I walk with my back to the sun and suddenly stop, the head of your shadow stubs itself against my feet. That doesn't matter, as long as it doesn't overshoot them. Tell me what you want.

TROILUS. I don't want anything.

HELEN. Tell me what you want, Troilus!

TROILUS. Everything! I want everything!

HELEN. You want everything. The moon?

TROILUS. Everything! Everything and more!

34

HELEN. You're beginning to talk like a real man already; you want to kiss me!

TROILUS. No!

HELEN. You want to kiss me, isn't that it, Troilus?

TROILUS. I would kill myself directly afterwards!

HELEN. Come nearer. How old are you?

TROILUS. Fifteen. Alas!

HELEN. Bravo that alas. Have you kissed girls of your own age?

TROILUS. I hate them.

HELEN. But you have kissed them?

TROILUS. Well, yes, you're bound to kiss them, you kiss them all. I would give my life not to have kissed any of them.

HELEN. You seem prepared to get rid of quite a number of lives. Why haven't you said to me frankly: Helen, I want to kiss you! I don't see anything wrong in your kissing me. Kiss me.

TROILUS. Never.

HELEN. And then, when the day came to an end, you would have come quietly to where I was sitting on the battlements watching the sun go down over the islands, and you would have turned my head towards you with your hands – from golden it would have become dark, only shadow now, you would hardly have been able to see me – and you would have kissed me, and I should have been very happy. Why this is Troilus, I should have said to myself: young Troilus is kissing me! Kiss me.

TROILUS. Never.

HELEN. I see. You think, once you have kissed me, you would hate me?

TROILUS. Oh! Older men have all the luck, knowing how to say what they want to!

HELEN. You say it well enough.

(*Enter* PARIS)

PARIS. Take care Helen, Troilus is a dangerous fellow.

HELEN. On the contrary. He wants to kiss me.

PARIS. Troilus, you know that if you kiss Helen, I shall kill you?

HELEN. Dying means nothing to him; no matter how often.

PARIS. What's the matter with him? Is he crouching to spring? Is he going to take a leap at you? He's too nice a boy. Kiss Helen, Troilus. I'll let you.

HELEN. If you can make up his mind to it you're cleverer than I am.

> (TROILUS *who was about to hurl himself on* HELEN *immediately draws back*)

PARIS. Listen, Troilus! Here's a committee of our revered elders coming to shut the Gates of War. Kiss Helen in front of them; it will make you famous. You want to be famous, don't you, later on in life?

TROILUS. No. I want nobody to have heard of me.

PARIS. You don't want to be famous? You don't want to be rich and powerful?

TROILUS. No. Poor. Ugly.

PARIS. Let me finish! So that you can have all the women you want.

TROILUS. I don't want any, none at all, none.

PARIS. Here come the senators! Now you can choose: either you kiss Helen in front of them, or I shall kiss her in front of you. Would you rather I did it? All right! Look! . . . Why, this was a new version of kiss you gave me, Helen. What was it?

HELEN. The kiss I had ready for Troilus.

PARIS. You don't know what you're missing, my boy! Are you leaving us? Goodbye, then.

HELEN. We shall kiss one another, Troilus. I'll answer for that.

> (TROILUS *goes*)

Troilus!

PARIS (*slightly unnerved*). You called very loudly, Helen.

> (*Enter* DEMOKOS)

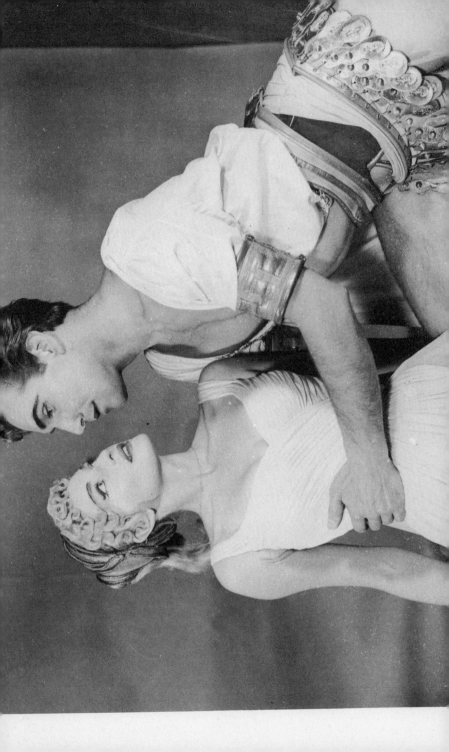

DEMOKOS. Helen, one moment! Look me full in the face. I've got here in my hand a magnificent bird which I'm going to set free. Are you looking? Here it is. Smooth back your hair, and smile a beautiful smile.

PARIS. I don't see how the bird will fly any better if Helen smooths her hair and gives a beautiful smile.

HELEN. It can't do me any harm, anyway.

DEMOKOS. Don't move. One! Two! Three! There! It's all over, you can go now.

HELEN. Where was the bird?

DEMOKOS. It's a bird who knows how to make himself invisible.

HELEN. Ask him next time to tell you how he does it.

(SHE *goes*)

PARIS. What is this nonsense?

DEMOKOS. I am writing a song on the subject of Helen's face. I needed to look at it closely, to engrave it, smiling, on my memory.

(*Enter* HECUBA, POLYXENE, ABNEOS, *the* MATHEMA-
TICIAN, *and some* OLD MEN)

HECUBA. Well, are you going to shut these Gates for us?

DEMOKOS. Certainly not. We might well have to open them again this very evening.

HECUBA. It is Hector's wish. And Hector will persuade Priam.

DEMOKOS. That is as we shall see. And what's more I have a surprise in store for Hector.

POLYXENE. Where do the Gates lead to, mama?

ABNEOS. To war, my child. When they are open it means there is war.

DEMOKOS. My friends . . .

HECUBA. War or not, it's an absurd symbolism, your Gate-way, and those two great doors always left open look very unsightly. All the dogs stop there.

MATHEMATICIAN. This is no domestic matter. It concerns war and the Gods.

HECUBA. Which is just as I said: the Gods never remember to shut their doors.

POLYXENE. I remember to shut them very well, don't I, mama?

PARIS. And you even include your fingers in them, don't you, my pretty one?

DEMOKOS. May I ask for a moment of silence, Paris? Abneos, and you, Mathematician, and you, my friends: I asked you to meet here earlier than the time fixed for the ceremony so that we could hold our first council. And it promises well that this first council of war should be, not a council of generals, but a council of intellectuals. For it isn't enough in war-time to have our soldiers drilled, well-armed, and spectacular. It is absolutely necessary to bring their enthusiasm up to fever pitch. The physical intoxication which their officers will get from them by a generous allowance of cheap wine supplied at the right moment, will still be ineffective against the Greeks, unless it is reinforced by the spiritual and moral intoxication which the poets can pour into them. If we are too old to fight we can at least make sure that the fighting is savage. I see you have something to say on the subject, Abneos.

ABNEOS. Yes. We must make a war-song.

DEMOKOS. Very proper. A war requires a war-song.

PARIS. We have done without one up to now.

HECUBA. War itself sings quite loud enough.

ABNEOS. We have done without one because up to now we were fighting only barbarians. It was nothing more than a hunt, and the hunting horn was all we needed. But now with the Greeks we're entering a different region of war altogether.

DEMOKOS. Exactly so, Abneos. The Greeks don't fight with everybody.

PARIS. We already have a national anthem.

ABNEOS. Yes. But it's a song of peace.

PARIS. If you sing a song of peace with enough gestures and grimaces it becomes a war-song. What are the words we have already?

ABNEOS. You know them perfectly well. There's no spirit in
them:
> 'We cut and bind the harvest,
> We tread the vineyard's blood.'

DEMOKOS. At the very most it's a war-song against farm
produce. You won't frighten the Spartans by threatening a
wheatfield.

PARIS. Sing it with a spear in your hand, and a dead body
at your feet, you will be surprised.

HECUBA. It includes the word 'blood', there's always that.

PARIS. The word 'harvest' as well. War rather approves of
the word 'harvest'.

ABNEOS. Why discuss it, when Demokos can invent an entirely
new one in a couple of hours.

DEMOKOS. A couple of hours is rather short.

HECUBA. Don't be afraid; it's more than you need for it. And
after the song will come the hymn, and after the hymn the
cantata. As soon as war is declared it will be impossible to
hold the poets back. Rhyme is still the most effective drum.

DEMOKOS. And the most useful, Hecuba: you don't know how
wisely you speak. I know war. As long as war isn't with us,
and the Gates are shut, each of us is free to insult it and
execrate it as we will. But once war comes, its pride and
autocracy is huge. You can gain its goodwill only by flattery
and adoration. So the mission of those who understand how
to speak and write is to compliment and praise war cease-
lessly and indiscriminately, otherwise we shut ourselves out
from his favour.

PARIS. Have you got an idea for your song already?

DEMOKOS. A marvellous idea, which no one will understand
better than you. War must be tired of the mask we always
give it, of Medusa's venomous hair and a Gorgon's lips.
I have had the notion to compare War's face with Helen's.
It will be enchanted by the comparison.

POLYXENE. What does War look like, mama?

HECUBA. Like your Aunt Helen.

POLYXENE. She is very pretty.

DEMOKOS. Then the discussion is closed. You can expect the war-song. Why are you looking worried, Mathematician?

MATHEMATICIAN. Because there are other things far more urgent than this war-song, far more urgent!

DEMOKOS. You think we should discuss the question of medals, false information, atrocity stories, and so on?

MATHEMATICIAN. I think we should discuss the insulting epithets.

HECUBA. The insulting epithets?

MATHEMATICIAN. Before they hurl their spears the Greek fighting-men hurl insults. You third cousin of a toad, they yell! You son of a sow! – They insult each other, like that! And they have a good reason for it. They know that the body is more vulnerable when self-respect has fled. Soldiers famous for their composure lose it immediately when they're treated as warts or maggots. We Trojans suffer from a grave shortage of insults.

DEMOKOS. The Mathematician is quite right. We are the only race in the world which doesn't insult its enemies before it kills them.

PARIS. You don't think it's enough that the civilians insult the enemy civilians?

MATHEMATICIAN. The armies have to show the same hatred the civilians do. You know what dissemblers armies can be in this way. Leave them to themselves and they spend their time admiring each other. Their front lines very soon become the only ranks of real brotherhood in the world. So naturally, when the theatre of war is so full of mutual consideration, hatred is driven back on to the schools, the salons, the trades-people. If our soldiers aren't at least equal to the Greeks in the fury of their epithets, they will lose all taste for insults and calumny, and as a natural consequence all taste for war.

DEMOKOS. Suggestion adopted! We will organize a cursing parade this evening.

PARIS. I should have thought they're big enough to find their own curses.

DEMOKOS. What a mistake! Could you, adroit as you are, find your own effective curses?

PARIS. I believe so.

DEMOKOS. You fool yourself. Come and stand face to face with Abneos and begin.

PARIS. Why Abneos?

DEMOKOS. Because he lends himself to this sort of thing, with his corpulence and one thing and another.

ABNEOS. Come on, then, speak up, you piece of pie-crust!

PARIS. No. Abneos doesn't inspire me. I'll start with you, if you don't mind.

DEMOKOS. With me? Certainly. You can let fly at ten paces. There we are. Begin.

HECUBA. Take a good look at him. You will be inspired.

PARIS. You old parasite! You filthy-footed iambic pentameter!

DEMOKOS. Just one second. To avoid any mistake you had better say who it is you're addressing.

PARIS. You're quite right! Demokos! Bloodshot bullock's eye! You fungus-ridden plum-tree!

DEMOKOS. Grammatically reasonable, but very naive. What is there in a fungus-ridden plum-tree to make me rise up foaming at the lips?

HECUBA. He also called you a bloodshot bullock's eye.

DEMOKOS. Bloodshot bullock's eye is better. But you see how you flounder, Paris? Search for something that can strike home to me. What are my faults, in your opinion?

PARIS. You are cowardly: your breath smells, and you have no talent.

DEMOKOS. You're asking for trouble!

PARIS. I was trying to please you.

POLYXENE. Why are we scolding Uncle Demokos, mama?

HECUBA. Because he is a cuckoo, dearest!

DEMOKOS. What did you say, Hecuba?

HECUBA. I was saying that you're a cuckoo, Demokos. If cuckoos had the absurdity, the affectation, the ugliness and the stench of vultures, you would be a cuckoo.

DEMOKOS. Wait a bit, Paris! Your mother is better at this than you are. Model yourselves on her. One hour's exercise each day for each soldier, and Hecuba has given us the superiority in insults which we badly need. As for the war-song, I'm not sure it wouldn't be wiser to entrust that to her as well.

HECUBA. If you like. But if so, I shouldn't say that war looks like Helen.

DEMOKOS. What would you say it looks like, in your opinion?

HECUBA. I will tell you when the Gates have been shut.

(*Enter* PRIAM, HECTOR, ANDROMACHE, *and presently* HELEN. *During the closing of the Gates,* ANDROMACHE *takes little* POLYXENE *aside and whispers a secret or an errand to her*)

HECTOR. As they nearly are.

DEMOKOS. One moment, Hector!

HECTOR. Aren't we ready to begin the ceremony?

HECUBA. Surely? The hinges are swimming in oil.

HECTOR. Well, then.

PRIAM. What our friends want you to understand, Hector, is that war is ready, too. Consider carefully. They're not mistaken. If you shut these Gates, in a minute we may have to open them again.

HECUBA. Even one minute of peace is worth taking.

HECTOR. Father, you should know what peace means to men who have been fighting for months. It's like solid ground to someone who was drowning or sinking in the quicksands. Do let us get our feet on to a few inches of peace, touch it, if only with the tips of our toes.

PRIAM. Hector: consider: inflicting the word peace on to the city today is as ruthless as though you gave it poison. You will take her off her guard, undermine her iron determination, debase, with the word peace, the accepted values of memory, affection, and hope. The soldiers will rush to buy the bread of peace, to drink the wine of peace, to hold in their arms the woman of peace, and in an hour you will put them back to face a war.

HECTOR. The war will never take place!

(*The sound of clamour near the Gates*)

DEMOKOS. No? Listen!

HECTOR. Shut the Gates. This is where we shall meet the Greeks. Conversation will be bitter enough as it is. We must receive them in peace.

PRIAM. My son, are we even sure we should let the Greeks disembark?

HECTOR. Disembark they shall. This meeting with Ulysses is our last chance of peace.

DEMOKOS. Disembark they shall not. Our honour is at stake. We shall be the laughing-stock of the whole world.

HECTOR. And you're taking it upon yourself to recommend to the Senate an action which would certainly mean war?

DEMOKOS. Upon myself? No, not at all. Will you come forward now, Busiris. This is where　ır mission begins.

HECTOR. Who is this stranger?

DEMOKOS. He is the greatest living expert on the rights of nations. It's a lucky chance he should be passing through Troy today. You can't say that he's a biased witness. He is neutral. Our Senate is willing to abide by his decision, a decision which all other nations will agree with tomorrow.

HECTOR. And what is your opinion?

BUSIRIS. My opinion, Princes, based on my own observation and further enquiry, is that the Greeks, in relation to Troy, are guilty of three breaches of international law. If you give them permission to disembark you will have sacrificed your position as the aggrieved party, and so lost the universal sympathy which would certainly have been yours in the conflict to follow.

HECTOR. Explain yourself.

BUSIRIS. Firstly, they have hoisted their flag hatchway and not masthead. A ship of war, my dear Princes and colleagues, hoists its flag hatchway only when replying to a salute from a boat carrying cattle. Clearly, then, so to salute a city and a city's population is an insult. As it happens, we have a precedent. Last year the Greeks hoisted their flag hatchway when they were entering the port of Orphea. The reply was incisive. Orphea declared war.

HECTOR. And what happened?

BUSIRIS. Orphea was beaten. Orphea no longer exists, nor the Orpheans either.

HECUBA. Perfect.

BUSIRIS. But the annihilation of a people doesn't alter in the least their superior moral position.

HECTOR. Go on.

BUSIRIS. Secondly, on entering your territorial waters the Greeks adopted the formation known as frontal. At the last congress there was some talk of including this formation in the paragraph of measures called defensive-aggressive. I was very happy to be able to get it restored under its proper heading of aggressive-defensive: so without doubt it is now one of the subtle forms of naval manœuvre which is a disguised form of blockade: that is to say, it constitutes a fault of the first degree! We have a precedent for this, as well. Five years ago the Greek navy adopted the frontal formation when they anchored outside Magnesia. Magnesia at once declared war.

HECTOR. Did they win it?

BUSIRIS. They lost it. There's not one stone of Magnesia still standing on another. But my redraft of the paragraph is still standing.

HECUBA. I congratulate you. We were beginning to be anxious.

HECTOR. Go on.

BUSIRIS. The third fault is not so serious. One of the Greek triremes has crept close in to shore without permission. Its captain, Ajax, the most unruly and impossible man among the Greeks, is climbing up towards the city, shouting scandal and provocation, and swearing he would like to kill Paris. But this is a very minor matter, from the international point of view; because it isn't, in any way, a formal breach of the law.

DEMOKOS. You have your information. The situation can only be resolved in one of two ways. To swallow an outrage, or return it. Choose.

HECTOR. Oneah, go and find Ajax. Head him off in this direction.

PARIS. I'm waiting here for him.

HECTOR. You will be good enough to stay in the Palace until I call for you. As for you, Busiris, you must understand that our city has no intention of being insulted by the Greeks.

BUSIRIS. I am not surprised. Troy's incorruptible pride is a legend all the world over.

HECTOR. You are going to provide me, here and now, with an argument which will allow our Senate to say that there has been no fault whatever on the part of our visitors, and with our pride untouched we welcome them here as our guests.

DEMOKOS. What nonsense is this?

BUSIRIS. It isn't in keeping with the facts, Hector.

HECTOR. My dear Busiris, all of us here know there's no better way of exercising the imagination than the study of law. No poet ever interpreted nature as freely as a lawyer interprets truth.

BUSIRIS. The Senate asked me for an opinion: I gave it.

HECTOR. And I ask you for an interpretation. An even subtler point of law.

BUSIRIS. It goes against my conscience.

HECTOR. Your conscience has seen Orphea destroyed, Magnesia destroyed: is it now contemplating, just as light-heartedly, the destruction of Troy?

HECUBA. Yes. He comes from Syracuse.

HECTOR. I do beg of you, Busiris. The lives of two countries depend on this. Help us.

BUSIRIS. Truth is the only help I can give you.

HECTOR. Precisely. Discover a truth which saves us. What is the use of justice if it doesn't hammer out a shield for innocent people? Forge us a truth. If you can't, there is one thing I can tell you, quite simply: we shall hold you here for as long as the war goes on.

BUSIRIS. What are you saying?

DEMOKOS. You're abusing your position, Hector!

HECUBA. During war we imprison the rights of man. There seems no reason why we shouldn't imprison a lawyer.

HECTOR. I mean what I say, Busiris. I've never failed yet to keep my promises, or my threats. And now either these guards are going to take you off to prison for a year or two, or else you leave here, this evening, heaped with gold. With this in mind, you can dispassionately examine the evidence once again.

BUSIRIS. Actually there are certain mitigating arguments.

HECTOR. I was sure there were.

BUSIRIS. In the case of the first fault, for instance, when the cattle-boat salute is given in certain seas where the shores are fertile, it could be interpreted as a salute from the sailors to the farmers.

HECTOR. That would be, in fact, the logical interpretation. The salute of the sea to the earth.

BUSIRIS. Not to mention that the cargo of cattle might easily be a cargo of bulls. In that case the homage would verge on flattery.

HECTOR. There you are. You've understood what I meant. We've arrived at our point of view.

BUSIRIS. And as to the frontal formation, that could as easily mean a promise as a provocation. Women wanting children give themselves not from the side but face to face.

HECTOR. Decisive argument.

BUSIRIS. Then, again, the Greek ships have huge carved nymphs for figureheads. A woman who comes towards you naked and open-armed is not a threat but an offer. An offer to talk, at any rate.

HECTOR. So there we have our honour safe and sound, Demokos. The next step is to make this consultation with Busiris public. Meanwhile, Minos, tell the port authorities to let Ulysses disembark without any loss of time.

DEMOKOS. It's no use even trying to discuss honour with these fighting men. They trade on the fact that you can't treat them as cowards.

MATHEMATICIAN. At any rate, Hector, deliver the Oration for the Dead. That will make you think again.

HECTOR. There's not going to be an Oration for the Dead.

PRIAM. But it's a part of the ceremony. The victorious general must always speak in honour of the dead when the Gates are closed.

HECTOR. An Oration for the Dead of a war is a hypocritical speech in defence of the living, a plea for acquittal. I am not so sure of my innocence.

DEMOKOS. The High Command is not responsible.

HECTOR. Alas, no one is: nor the Gods either. Besides, I have given my oration for the dead already. I gave it to them in their last minute of life, when they were lying on the battle-field, on a little slope of olive-trees, while they could still attend me with what was left of their sight and hearing. I can tell you what I said to them. There was one, disembowelled, already turning up the whites of his eyes, and I said to him: 'It's not so bad, you know, it's not so bad; you will do all right, old man'. And one with his skull split in two; I said: 'You look pretty comical with that broken nose'. And my little equerry, with his left arm hanging useless and his last blood flowing out of him; and I said, 'It's a good thing for you it's the left arm you've splintered'. I am happy I gave them one final swig of life; it was all they asked for; they died drinking it. And there's nothing else to be said. Shut the Gates.

POLYXENE. Did the little equerry die, as well?

HECTOR. Yes, puss-cat. He died. He stretched out his right arm. Someone I couldn't see took him by his perfect hand. And then he died.

DEMOKOS. Our general seems to confuse remarks made to the dying with the Oration for the Dead.

PRIAM. Why must you be so stubborn, Hector?

HECTOR. Very well: you shall have the Oration. (*He takes a position below the gates*) – You who cannot hear us, who cannot see us, listen to these words, look at those who come to honour you. We have won the war. I know that's of no moment to you. You are the victors, too. But we are victorious, and still live. That's where the difference is between us and why I'm ashamed. I don't know whether, among the crowd of the dead, any privilege is given to men who died victorious. But the living, whether victorious or not, have privilege enough. We have our eyes. We see the sun. We do what all men do under the sun. We eat. We drink. By the moon, we sleep with our wives. And with yours, now you have gone.

DEMOKOS. You insult the dead!

HECTOR. Do you think so?

DEMOKOS. Either the dead or the living.

HECTOR. There is a distinction.

PRIAM. Come to the peroration, Hector. The Greeks are coming ashore.

HECTOR. I will come to it now . . . Breathe in this incense, touch these offerings, you who can neither smell nor touch. And understand, since I speak to you sincerely, I haven't an equal tenderness and respect for all of you. Though all of you are the dead, with you as with us who survive there are men of courage and men of fear, and you can't make me confuse, for the sake of a ceremony, the dead I admire with those I can't admire. But what I have to say to you today is that war seems to me the most sordid, hypocritical way of making all men equal: and I accept death neither as a punishment or expiation for the coward, nor as a reward to the living. So, whatever you may be, absent, forgotten, purposeless, unresting, without existence, one thing is certain when we close these Gates: we must ask you to forgive us, we, the deserters who survive you, who feel we have stolen two great privileges, I hope the sound of their names will never reach you: the warmth of the living body, and the sky.

POLYXENE. The gates are shutting, mama!

HECUBA. Yes, darling.

POLYXENE. The dead men are pushing them shut.

HECUBA. They help, a little.

POLYXENE. They're helping quite a lot, especially over on the right.

HECTOR. Is it done? Are they shut?

GUARD. Tight as a clam.

HECTOR. We're at peace, father, we're at peace.

HECUBA. We're at peace!

POLYXENE. It feels much better, doesn't it, mama?

HECTOR. Indeed it does.

POLYXENE. I feel much better, anyway.

(*The sound of the* GREEKS' *music*)

A MESSENGER. The Greeks have landed, Priam!

DEMOKOS. What music! What frightful music! It's the most anti-Trojan music there could possibly be! Let's go and give them a welcome to match it.

HECTOR. Receive them royally, bring them here safely. You are responsible.

MATHEMATICIAN. At any rate we ought to counter with some Trojan music. Hector, if we can't be indignant any other way, you can authorize a battle of music.

CROWD. The Greeks! The Greeks!

MESSENGER. Ulysses is on the landing-stage, Priam. Where are we to take him?

PRIAM. Conduct him here. Send word to us in the palace when he comes. Keep with us, Paris. We don't want you too much in evidence just yet.

HECTOR. Let's go and prepare what we shall say to the Greeks, father.

DEMOKOS. You'd better prepare it somewhat better than your speech for the dead; you're likely to meet more contradiction.

(*Exeunt* PRIAM *and his* SONS)

If you are going with them, tell us before you go, Hecuba, what it is you think war looks like.

HECUBA. You insist on knowing?

DEMOKOS. If you've seen what it looks like, tell us.

HECUBA. Like the bottom of a baboon. When the baboon is up in a tree, with its hind end facing us, there is the face of war exactly: scarlet, scaley, glazed, framed in a clotted, filthy wig.

DEMOKOS. So he has two faces: this you describe, and Helen's.

(*Exit*)

ANDROMACHE. Here is Helen now. Polyxene, you remember what you have to say to her?

POLYXENE. Yes.

ANDROMACHE. Go to her, then.

(*Enter* HELEN)

HELEN. Do you want to talk to me, darling?

POLYXENE. Yes, Aunt Helen.

HELEN. It must be important, you're so very tense.

POLYXENE. Yes, Aunt Helen.

HELEN. Is it something you can't tell me without standing so stiffly?

POLYXENE. No, Aunt Helen.

HELEN. Do tell me, then; you make me feel terrible when you stand there like a little stick.

POLYXENE. Aunt Helen, if you love anyone, please go away.

HELEN. Why should I go away, darling?

POLYXENE. Because of the war.

HELEN. Do you know about war already, then?

POLYXENE. I don't exactly know about it. I think it means we have to die.

HELEN. And do you know what dying is?

POLYXENE. I don't exactly. I think it means we don't feel anything any more.

HELEN. What exactly was it that Andromache told you to ask me?

POLYXENE. If you love us at all, please to go away.

HELEN. That doesn't seem to me very logical. If you loved someone you wouldn't leave them?

POLYXENE. Oh, no! Never!

HELEN. Which would you rather do: go right away from Hecuba, or never feel anything any more?

POLYXENE. Oh, never feel anything! I would rather stay, and never feel anything any more.

HELEN. You see how badly you put things to me. If I'm to leave you, I mustn't love you. Would you rather I didn't love you?

POLYXENE. Oh, no! I want you to love me.

HELEN. In other words, you didn't know what you were saying, did you?

POLYXENE. No.

HECUBA (*offstage*). Polyxene!

(*Enter* HECUBA)

Are you deaf, Polyxene? Why did you shut your eyes when you saw me? Are you playing at being a statue? Come with me.

HELEN. She is teaching herself not to feel anything. But she has no gift for it.

HECUBA. Can you hear me, Polyxene? And see me?

POLYXENE. Yes, I can hear you. I can see you, too.

HECUBA. Why are you crying? Don't you like to see and hear me?

POLYXENE. If I do, you will go away.

HECUBA. I think it would be better, Helen, if you left Polyxene alone. She is too sensitive to touch the insensitive, even through your beautiful dress and your beautiful voice.

HELEN. I quite agree with you. I advise Andromache to carry her own messages. Kiss me, Polyxene. I shall go away this evening, since that is what you would like.

POLYXENE. Don't go! Don't go!

HELEN. Bravo! You are quite loosened up again!

HECUBA. Are you coming with us, Andromache?

ANDROMACHE. No: I shall wait here.

(*Exeunt* HECUBA *and* POLYXENE)

HELEN. You want an explanation?

ANDROMACHE. I believe it's necessary.

HELEN. Listen to the way they're shouting and arguing down below. Isn't that enough? Do you and I have to have explanations, too? And what explanations, since I'm leaving here anyway?

ANDROMACHE. Whether you go or stay isn't any longer the problem.

HELEN. Tell Hector that. You will make his day easier.

ANDROMACHE. Yes, Hector is obsessed by the thought of getting you away. All men are the same. They take no notice of the stag in the thicket because they're already chasing the hare. Perhaps men can hunt like that. But not the gods.

HELEN. If you have discovered what the gods are after in this affair, I congratulate you.

ANDROMACHE. I don't know that the gods are after anything. But there is something the universe is after. Ever since this morning, it seems to me, everything has begged and cried out for it, men, animals, even the leaves on the trees and my own child, not yet born.

HELEN. Cried out for what?

ANDROMACHE. That you should love Paris.

HELEN. If they know so certainly that I don't love Paris, they are better informed than I am.

ANDROMACHE. But you don't love him! You could love him, perhaps. But, at present, you are both living in a misunderstanding.

HELEN. I live with him happily, amicably, in complete agreement. We understand each other so well, I don't really see how this can be called a misunderstanding.

ANDROMACHE. Agreement is never reached in love. The life of a wife and husband who love each other is never at rest. Whether the marriage is true or false, the marriage portion is the same: elemental discord. Hector is my absolute opposite. He shares none of my tastes. We pass our days either getting the better of one another, or sacrificing ourselves. There is no tranquillity for lovers.

HELEN. And if I went pale whenever I saw Paris: and my eyes filled with tears, and the palms of my hands were moist, you think Menelaus would be delighted, and the Greeks pleased and quite satisfied?

ANDROMACHE. It wouldn't much matter then what the Greeks thought.

HELEN. And the war would never happen?

ANDROMACHE. Perhaps, indeed, it would never happen. Perhaps if you loved him, love would call to the rescue one of its own equals: generosity or intelligence. No one, not even destiny itself, attacks devotion lightheartedly. And even if the war did happen, why, I think even then ——

HELEN. Then it wouldn't be the same war, I suppose.

ANDROMACHE. Oh, no, Helen! You know what this struggle is going to be. Fate would never take so many precautions for an ordinary quarrel. It means to build the future on this war, the future of our countries and our peoples, and our ways of thinking. It won't be so bad if our thoughts and our future are built on the story of a man and a woman who truly love each other. But fate hasn't noticed yet that you are lovers only on paper, officially. To think that we're going to suffer and die only for a pair of theoretical lovers: and the splendour and calamity of the age to come will be founded on a trivial adventure between two people who don't love each other – that's what is so horrible.

HELEN. If everybody thinks that we love each other, it comes to the same thing.

ANDROMACHE. They don't think so. But no one will admit that he doesn't. Everyone, when there's war in the air, learns to live in a new element: falsehood. Everybody lies. Our old men don't worship beauty: they worship themselves, they worship ugliness. And this indignation the Greeks are showing us is a lie. God knows, they're amused enough at what you can do with Paris! Their boats, in the bay, with their patriotic anthems and their streamers flying, are a falsehood of the sea. And Hector's life and my son's life, too, are going to be played out in hypocrisy and pretence.

HELEN. So?

ANDROMACHE. I beg of you, Helen. You see how I'm pressed against you as though I were begging you to love me. Love Paris! Or tell me that I'm mistaken! Tell me that you would kill yourself if Paris were to die! Tell me that you would even let yourself be disfigured if it would keep him alive. Then the war will only be a scourge, not an injustice.

HELEN. You are being very difficult. I don't think my way of loving is as bad as all that. Certainly I don't get upset and ill when Paris leaves me to play bowls or go fishing for eels. But I do feel commanded by him, magnetically attracted. Magnetism is a kind of love, as much as devotion. And it's an old and fruitful passion in its own way, as desperate devotion and passionate weeping are in theirs. I'm as content in this love as a star in a constellation. It's my own centre of gravity; I shine there; it's the way I breathe, and the way I take life in my arms. And it's easy to see what sons this love can produce: tall, clear-cut boys, of great distinction, with fine fingers and short noses. What will it all become if I fill it with jealousy, with emotion, and anxiety? The world is nervous enough already: look at yourself!

ANDROMACHE. Fill it with pity, Helen. That's the only help the world needs.

HELEN. There we are; I knew it would come; the word has been said.

ANDROMACHE. What word?

HELEN. The word 'pity'. You must talk to someone else. I'm afraid I'm not very good at pity.

ANDROMACHE. Because you don't know unhappiness.

HELEN. Maybe. It could also be that I think of unhappy people as my equals, I accept them, and I don't think of my health and my position and beauty as any better than their misery. It's a sense of brotherhood I have.

ANDROMACHE. You're blaspheming, Helen.

HELEN. I am sure people pity others to the same extent that they would pity themselves. Unhappiness and ugliness are mirrors they can't bear to look into. I haven't any pity for myself. You will see, if war breaks out. I'll put up with hunger and pain better than you will. And insults, too. Do you think I don't hear what the Trojan women say when I'm going past them? They treat me like a slut. They say that the morning light shows me up for what they think me. It may be true, or it may not be. It doesn't matter to me, one way or the other.

ANDROMACHE. Stop, Helen!

HELEN. And of course I can see, in what your husband called the coloured picture-book in my head, pictures of Helen grown old, flabby, toothless, sitting hunched-up in the kitchen, sucking sweets. I can see the white enamel I've plastered over my wrinkles, and the bright colours the sweets are, very clearly. But it leaves me completely indifferent.

ANDROMACHE. I am lost.

HELEN. Why? If you're content with one perfect couple to make the war acceptable, there is always you and Hector, Andromache.

(*Enter* AJAX, *then* HECTOR)

AJAX. Where is he? Where's he hiding himself? A coward! A typical Trojan!

HECTOR. Who are you looking for?

AJAX. I'm looking for Paris.

HECTOR. I am his brother.

AJAX. Beautiful family! I am Ajax! What's your name?

HECTOR. My name's Hector.

AJAX. It ought to be pimp!

HECTOR. I see that Greece has sent over her diplomats. What do you want?

AJAX. War.

HECTOR. Not a hope. Why do you want it?

AJAX. Your brother carried off Helen.

HECTOR. I am told she was willing.

AJAX. A Greek woman can do what she likes. She doesn't have to ask permission from you. He carried her off. It's a reason for war.

HECTOR. We can offer our apologies.

AJAX. What's a Trojan apology? We're not leaving here without your declaration of war.

HECTOR. Declare it yourselves.

AJAX. All right, we will. As from this evening.

HECTOR. That's a lie. You won't declare war. There isn't an island in the archipelego that will back you if we aren't in any way responsible. And we don't intend to be.

AJAX. Will you declare it yourself, personally, if I call you a coward?

HECTOR. That is a name I accept.

AJAX. I've never known such unmilitary reaction! Suppose I tell you what the people of Greece thinks of Troy, that Troy is a cess-pit of vice and stupidity?

HECTOR. Troy is obstinate. You won't get your war.

AJAX. Suppose I spit on her?

HECTOR. Spit.

AJAX. Suppose I strike you, you, one of her princes?

HECTOR. Try it.

AJAX. Suppose I slap your face, you disgusting example of Troy's conceit and her spurious honour?

HECTOR. Strike.

AJAX (*striking him*). There. If this lady's your wife she must be proud of you.

HECTOR. I know her. She is proud.

(*Enter* DEMOKOS)

DEMOKOS. What's all the noise about? What does this drunkard want, Hector?

HECTOR. He has got what he wants.

DEMOKOS. What is going on, Andromache?

ANDROMACHE. Nothing.

AJAX. Two times nothing. A Greek hits Hector, and Hector puts up with it.

DEMOKOS. Is this true, Hector?

HECTOR. Completely false, isn't it, Helen?

HELEN. The Greeks are great liars. Greek men, I mean.

AJAX. Is it natural for him to have one cheek redder than the other?

HECTOR. Yes. I am healthier on that side.

DEMOKOS. Tell the truth, Hector. Has he dared to raise his hand against you?

HECTOR. That is my concern.

DEMOKOS. It's the concern of war. You are the figurehead of Troy.

HECTOR. Exactly. No one is going to slap a figurehead.

DEMOKOS. Who are you, you brute? I am Demokos, second son of Achichaos!

AJAX. The second son of Achichaos? How do you do? Tell me: is it as serious to slap a second son of Achichaos as to strike Hector?

DEMOKOS. Quite as serious, you drunk. I am the head of the senate. If you want war, war to the death, you have only to try.

AJAX. All right. I'll try. (*He slaps* DEMOKOS)

DEMOKOS. Trojans! Soldiers! To the rescue!

HECTOR. Be quiet, Demokos!

DEMOKOS. To arms! Troy's been insulted! Vengeance!

HECTOR. Be quiet, I tell you.

DEMOKOS. I *will* shout! I'll rouse the city!

HECTOR. Be quiet! If you won't, I shall hit you, too!

DEMOKOS. Priam! Anchises! Come and see the shame of Troy burning on Hector's face!

(HECTOR *strikes* DEMOKOS. AJAX *laughs. During the scene,* PRIAM *and his lords group themselves ready to receive* ULYSSES)

PRIAM. What are you shouting for, Demokos?

DEMOKOS. I have been struck.

AJAX. Go and complain to Achichaos!

PRIAM. Who struck you?

DEMOKOS. Hector! Ajax! Ajax! Hector!

PARIS. What is he talking about? He's mad!

HECTOR. Nobody struck him, did they, Helen?

HELEN. I was watching most carefully, and I didn't notice anything.

AJAX. Both his cheeks are the same colour.

PARIS. Poets often get upset for no reason. It's what they call their inspiration. We shall get a new national anthem out of it.

DEMOKOS. You will pay for this, Hector.

VOICES. Ulysses! Here is Ulysses!

(AJAX *goes amicably to* HECTOR)

AJAX. Well done. Plenty of pluck. Noble adversary. A beautiful hit.

HECTOR. I did my best.

AJAX. Excellent method, too. Straight elbow. The wrist on an angle. Safe position for the carpus and metacarpus. Your slap must be stronger than mine is.

HECTOR. I doubt it.

AJAX. You must be able to throw a javelin magnificently with this iron forearm and this shoulder-bone for a pivot.

HECTOR. Eighty yards.

AJAX. My deepest respect! My dear Hector, forgive me. I withdraw my threats, I take back my slap. We have enemies in common, in the sons of Achichaos. I won't fight with anybody who shares with me an enmity for the sons of Achichaos. Not another mention of war. I don't know what Ulysses has got in mind, but count on me to arrange the whole thing.

(*He goes towards* ULYSSES *and comes back with him*)

ANDROMACHE. I love you, Hector.

HECTOR (*Showing his cheek*). Yes; but don't kiss me just yet.

ANDROMACHE. You have won this round, as well. Be confident.

HECTOR. I win every round. But still with each victory the prize escapes me.

ULYSSES. Priam and Hector?

PRIAM. Yes. And behind us, Troy, and the suburbs of Troy, and the land of Troy, and the Hellespont.

ULYSSES. I am Ulysses.

PRIAM. This is Anchises.

ULYSSES. There are many people here for a diplomatic conversation.

PRIAM. And here is Helen.

ULYSSES. Good morning, my queen.

HELEN. I've grown younger here, Ulysses. I've become a princess again.

PRIAM. We are ready to listen to you.

AJAX. Ulysses, you speak to Priam. I will speak to Hector.

ULYSSES. Priam, we have come to take Helen home again.

AJAX. You do understand, don't you, Hector? We can't have things happening like this.

ULYSSES. Greece and Menelaus cry out for vengeance.

AJAX. If deceived husbands can't cry out for vengeance, what can they do?

ULYSSES. Deliver Helen over to us within an hour. Otherwise it means war.

HECTOR. But if we give Helen back to you give us your assurance there will be peace.

AJAX. Utter tranquillity.

HECTOR. If she goes on board within an hour, the matter is closed.

AJAX. And all is forgotten.

HECTOR. I think there's no doubt we can come to an understanding, can we not, Helen?

HELEN. Yes, no doubt.

ULYSSES. You don't mean to say that Helen is being given back to us?

HECTOR. Exactly that. She is ready.

AJAX. What about her baggage? She is sure to have more to take back than when she came.

HECTOR. We return her to you, bag and baggage, and you guarantee peace. No reprisals, no vengeance!

AJAX. A woman is lost, a woman is found, and we're back where we were. Perfect! Isn't it, Ulysses?

ULYSSES. Just wait a moment. I guarantee nothing. Before we say there are going to be no reprisals we have to be sure there has been no cause for reprisals. We have to make sure

that Menelaus will find Helen exactly as she was when she
was taken from him.

HECTOR. How is he going to discover any difference?

ULYSSES. A husband is very perceptive when a world-wide
scandal has put him on his guard. Paris will have had to have
respected Helen. And if that isn't so . . .

CROWD. Oh, no! It isn't so!

ONE VOICE. Not exactly!

HECTOR. And if it is so?

ULYSSES. Where is this leading us, Hector?

HECTOR. Paris has not touched Helen. They have both taken
me into their confidence.

ULYSSES. What is this absurd story?

HECTOR. The true story, isn't it, Helen?

HELEN. Why does it seem to you so extraordinary?

A VOICE. It's terrible! It puts us to shame!

HECTOR. Why do you have to smile, Ulysses? Do you see the
slightest indication in Helen that she has failed in her
duty?

ULYSSES. I'm not looking for one. Water leaves more mark
on a duck's back than dishonour does on a woman.

PARIS. You're speaking to a queen.

ULYSSES. Present queens excepted, naturally. So, Paris, you
have carried off this queen, carried her off naked; and I
imagine that you didn't go into the water wearing all your
armour; and yet you weren't seized by any taste or desire
for her?

PARIS. A naked queen is dressed in her dignity.

HELEN. She has only to remember to keep it on.

ULYSSES. How long did the voyage last? I took three days
with my ships, which are faster than yours.

VOICES. What are these intolerable insults to the Trojan navy?

A VOICE. Your winds are faster! Not your ships!

ULYSSES. Let us say three days, if you like. Where was the
queen during those three days?

PARIS. Lying down on the deck.

ULYSSES. And Paris was where? In the crow's nest?

HELEN. Lying beside me.

ULYSSES. Was he reading as he lay beside you? Or fishing for goldfish?

HELEN. Sometimes he fanned me.

ULYSSES. Without ever touching you?

HELEN. One day, the second day, I think it was, he kissed my hand.

ULYSSES. Your hand! I see. An outbreak of the animal in him.

HELEN. I thought it was more dignified to take no notice.

ULYSSES. The rolling of the ship didn't throw you towards each other? I don't think it's an insult to the Trojan navy to suggest that its ships roll?

A VOICE. They roll much less than the Greek ships pitch!

AJAX. Pitch? Our Greek ships? If they seem to be pitching it's because of their high prows and their scooped-out sterns!

A VOICE. Oh, yes! The arrogant face and the flat behind, that's Greek all right.

ULYSSES. And what about the three nights you were sailing? The stars appeared and vanished again three times over the pair of you. Do you remember nothing of those three nights?

HELEN. I don't know. Oh, yes! I'd forgotten. I learnt a lot more about the stars.

ULYSSES. While you were asleep, perhaps, he might have taken you . . .

HELEN. A mosquito can wake me.

HECTOR. They will both swear to you, if you like, by our goddess Aphrodite.

ULYSSES. We can do without that. I know what Aphrodite is. Her favourite oath is a perjury. – It's a curious story you're telling me: and it will certainly destroy the idea that the rest of the Archipelego has always had of the Trojans.

PARIS. Why, what do they think of us in the Archipelego?

ULYSSES. You're thought of as less accomplished at trading than we are, but handsome and irresistible. Go on with your story, Paris. It's an interesting contribution to the study of human behaviour. What good reason could you have possibly had for respecting Helen when you had her at your mercy?

PARIS. I . . . I loved her.

HELEN. If you don't know what love is, Ulysses, I shouldn't venture on the subject.

ULYSSES. You must admit, Helen, you would never have followed him if you had known the Trojans were impotent.

VOICES. Shame! Muzzle him! Bring your women here, and you'll soon see! And your grandmother!

ULYSSES. I expressed myself badly. I meant that Paris, the handsome Paris, is impotent.

A VOICE. Why don't you say something, Paris? Are you going to make us the laughing-stock of the world?

PARIS. Hector, you can see, this is a most unpleasant situation for me!

HECTOR. You have to put up with it only a few minutes longer. Goodbye, Helen. And I hope your virtue will become as proverbial as your frailty might have done.

HELEN. That doesn't worry me. The centuries always give us the recognition we deserve.

ULYSSES. Paris the impotent, that's a very good surname! If you care to, Helen, you can kiss him for once.

PARIS. Hector!

FIRST TOPMAN. Are you going to tolerate this farce, commander?

HECTOR. Be quiet! I am in charge here!

TOPMAN. And a rotten job you make of it! We've stood quite enough. We'll tell you, we, Paris's own seamen, we'll tell you what he did with your queen!

VOICES. Bravo! Tell him!

TOPMAN. He's sacrificing himself on his brother's orders. I was an officer on board his ship. I saw everything.

HECTOR. You were quite wrong.

TOPMAN. Do you think a Trojan sailor doesn't know what he sees? I can tell the sex of a seagull thirty yards off. Come over here, Olpides. Olpides was up in the crow's nest. He saw everything from on top. I was standing on the stairs in the hatchway. My head was exactly on a level with them, like a cat on the end of a bed. Shall I tell him, Trojans?

HECTOR. Silence!

VOICES. Tell him! Go on and tell him!

TOPMAN. And they hadn't been on board more than two minutes, wasn't that true, Olpides?

OLPIDES. Only time enough for the queen to dry herself, being just come up out of the water, and to comb the parting into her hair again. I could see her parting, from her forehead over to the nape of her neck, from where I was.

TOPMAN. And he sent us all down into the hold, except the two of us who he couldn't see.

OLPIDES. And without a pilot, the ship drifted due north. There was no wind, and yet the sails were bellied out full.

TOPMAN. And when I looked out from where I was hiding, what I should have seen was the outline of one body, but what I did see was in the shape of two, like a wheaten loaf and rye bread, baking in the oven together.

OLPIDES. But from up where I was, I more often saw one body than two, but sometimes it was white, and sometimes it was golden brown.

TOPMAN. So much for impotence! And as for respectful, inexpressive love, and unspoken affection, you tell him, Olpides, what you heard from your ledge up there! Women's voices carry upwards, men's voice stay on the ground. I shall tell you what Paris said.

OLPIDES. She call him her ladybird, her little ewe-lamb.

TOPMAN. And he called her his lion, his panther. They reversed the sexes. Because they were being so affectionate. It's not unusual.

OLPIDES. And then she said: 'You are my darling oak-tree, I put my arms round you as if you were an oak-tree'. When you're at sea you think about trees, I suppose.

TOPMAN. And he called her his birch-tree: 'My trembling silver birch-tree!' I remember the word birch-tree very well. It's a Russian tree.

OLPIDES. And I had to stay up in the crow's nest all night. You don't half get thirsty up there, and hungry, and everything else.

TOPMAN. And when at last they got up from the deck to go to bed they swayed on their feet. And that's how your wife Penelope would have got on with Trojan impotence.

VOICES. Bravo! Bravo!

A WOMAN'S VOICE. All praise to Paris.

A JOVIAL MAN. Render to Paris what belongs to Paris!

HECTOR. This is a pack of lies, isn't it, Helen?

ULYSSES. Helen is listening enraptured.

HELEN. I forgot they were talking about me. They sound so wonderfully convincing.

ULYSSES. Do you dare to say they are lying, Paris?

PARIS. In some of the particulars, yes, I think they are.

TOPMAN. We're not lying, either in the general or the particular. Are we, Olpides? Do you deny the expressions of love you used? Do you deny the word panther?

PARIS. Not especially the word panther.

TOPMAN. Well, birch-tree, then? I see. It's the phrase 'trembling silver birch-tree' that embarrasses you. Well, like it or not, you used it. I swear you used it, and anyway what is there to blush about in the word 'birch-tree'? I have seen these silver birch-trees trembling against the snow in wintertime, by the shores of the Caspian, with their rings of black bark apparently separated by rings of space, so that you wondered what was carrying the branches. And I've seen them at the height of summer, beside the canal at Astrakhan, with their white rings like fresh mushrooms. And the leaves talked and made signs to me. To see them quivering, gold above and silver underneath, it makes your heart melt! I could have wept like a woman, isn't that true, Olpides? That's how I feel about the birch-tree.

CROWD. Bravo! Bravo!

ANOTHER SAILOR. And it wasn't only the topman and Olpides who saw them, Priam. The entire crew came wriggling up through the hatches and peering under the handrails. The whole ship was one great spy-glass.

THIRD SAILOR. Spying out love.

ULYSSES. There you have it, Hector!

HECTOR. Be quiet, the lot of you.

TOPMAN. Well, keep this quiet, if you can!

(IRIS *appears in the sky*)

PEOPLE. Iris! Iris!

PARIS. Has Aphrodite sent you?

IRIS. Yes, Aphrodite sent me, and told me that I should say to you that love is the world's chief law. Whatever strengthens love becomes in itself sacred, even falsehood, avarice, or luxury. She takes all lovers under her protection, from the king to the goat-herd. And she forbids both of you, Hector and Ulysses, to separate Paris from Helen. Or else there will be war.

PARIS AND THE OLD MEN. Thank you, Iris.

HECTOR. Is there any message from Pallas Athene?

IRIS. Yes; Pallas Athene told me that I should say to you that reason is the chief law of the world. All who are lovers, she wishes me to say, are out of their minds. She would like you to tell her quite frankly what is more ridiculous than the mating of cocks with hens or flies with flies. And she orders both of you, Hector, and Ulysses, to separate Helen from this Paris of the curly hair. Or else there will be war.

HECTOR AND THE WOMEN. Thank you, Iris!

PRIAM. Oh, my son, it isn't Aphrodite nor Pallas Athene who rules the world. What is it Zeus commands us to do in this time of uncertainty?

IRIS. Zeus, the master of the Gods, told me that I should say to you that those who see in the world nothing but love are as foolish as those who cannot see it at all. It is wise, Zeus, master of the Gods informs you, it is wise sometimes to make love, and at other times not to make love. The decision he gives to Hector and Ulysses, is to separate Helen and Paris without separating them. He orders all the rest of you to go away and leave the negotiators to face each other. And let them so arrange matters that there will be no war. Or else – he swears to you: he swears there will be war.

(*Exit* IRIS)

HECTOR. At your service, Ulysses!

ULYSSES. At your service.

(ALL *withdraw*)

(*A great rainbow is seen in the sky*)

HELEN. How very like Iris to leave her scarf behind.

HECTOR. Now we come to the real tussle, Ulysses.

ULYSSES. Yes: out of which either war or peace is going to come.

HECTOR. Will war come of it?

ULYSSES. We shall know in five minutes time.

HECTOR. If it's to be a battle of words, my chances are small.

ULYSSES. I believe it will be more a battle of weight. It's as though we were one on each side of a pair of scales. How we weigh in the balance will be what counts in the end.

HECTOR. How we weigh in the balance? And what is my weight, Ulysses? My weight is a young man, a young woman, an unborn child. Joy of life, belief in life, a response to whatever's natural and good.

ULYSSES. And my weight is the mature man, the wife thirty-five years old, the son whose height I measure each month with notches against the doorpost of the palace. My weight is the pleasures of living, and a mistrust of life.

HECTOR. Hunting, courage, loyalty, love.

ULYSSES. Circumspection in the presence of the gods, of men, and everything else.

HECTOR. The Phrygian oak-tree, all the leafy, thick-set oak-trees that grow on our hills with our curly-coated oxen.

ULYSSES. The power and wisdom of the olive-tree.

HECTOR. I weigh the hawk, I look straight into the sun.

ULYSSES. I weigh the owl.

HECTOR. I weigh the whole race of humble peasants, hard-working craftsmen, thousands of ploughs and looms, forges and anvils . . . Why is it, when I put all these in the scale in front of you, all at once they seem to me to weigh so light?

ULYSSES. I am the weight of this incorruptible, unpitying air of these coasts and islands.

HECTOR. Why go on? The scales have tipped.

ULYSSES. To my side? Yes, I think so.

HECTOR. And you want war?

ULYSSES. I don't want it. But I'm less sure whether war may not want us.

HECTOR. Our peoples have brought us together to prevent it. Our meeting itself shows that there is still some hope.

ULYSSES. You are young, Hector! It's usual on the eve of every war, for the two leaders of the peoples concerned to meet privately at some innocent village, on a terrace in a garden overlooking a lake. And they decide together that war is the world's worst scourge, and as they watch the rippling reflections in the water, with magnolia petals dropping on to their shoulders, they are both of them peace-loving, modest and friendly. They study one another. They look into each other's eyes. And, warmed by the sun and mellowed by the claret, they can't find anything in the other man's face to justify hatred, nothing, indeed, which doesn't inspire human affection, nothing incompatible in their languages any more, or in their particular way of scratching the nose or drinking wine. They really are exuding peace, and the world's desire for peace. And when their meeting is over, they shake hands in a most sincere brotherly fashion, and turn to smile and wave as they drive away. And the next day war breaks out. And so it is with us both at this moment. Our peoples, who have drawn aside, saying nothing while we have this interview, are not expecting us to win a victory over the inevitable. They have merely given us full powers, isolated here together, to stand above the catastrophe and taste the essential brotherhood of enemies. Taste it. It's a rare dish. Savour it. But that is all. One of the privileges of the great is to witness catastrophes from a terrace.

HECTOR. Do you think this is a conversation between enemies we are having?

ULYSSES. I should say a duet before the full orchestra. Because we have been created sensible and courteous, we can talk to each other, an hour or so before the war, in the

way we shall talk to each other long after it's over, like old
antagonists. We are merely having our reconciliation before
the struggle instead of after it. That may be unwise. If one
day one of us should have to kill the other, it might be as
well if it wasn't a friend's face we recognized as the body
dropped to the ground. But, as the universe well knows, we
are going to fight each other.

HECTOR. The universe might be mistaken. One way to
recognize error is the fact that it's universal.

ULYSSES. Let's hope so. But when destiny has brought up
two nations, as for years it has brought up yours and mine,
to a future of similar invention and authority, and given to
each a different scale of values (as you and I saw just now,
when we weighed pleasure against pleasure, conscience
against conscience, even nature itself against nature): when
the nation's architects and poets and painters have created
for them opposing kingdoms of sound, and form, and
subtlety, when we have a Trojan tile roof, a Theban arch,
Phrygian red, Greek blue: the universe knows that destiny
wasn't preparing alternative ways for civilization to flower.
It was contriving the dance of death, letting loose the
brutality and human folly which is all that the gods are really
contented by. It's a mean way to contrive things, I agree.
But we are Heads of State, you and I; we can say this
between ourselves: it is Destiny's way of contriving things,
inevitably.

HECTOR. And this time it has chosen to match Greece with Troy?

ULYSSES. This morning I was still in doubt. As soon as I
stepped on to your landing stage I was certain of it.

HECTOR. You mean you felt yourself on enemy soil?

ULYSSES. Why will you always harp on the word enemy?
Born enemies don't fight. Nations you would say were
designed to go to war against each other – by their skins,
their language, their smell: always jealous of each other,
always hating each other – they're not the ones who fight.
You will find the real antagonists in nations fate has groomed
and made ready for the same war.

HECTOR. And you think we have been made ready for the Greek war?

ULYSSES. To an astonishing extent. Just as nature, when she foresees a struggle between two kinds of insects, equips them with weaknesses and weapons which correspond, so we, living well apart, unknown to ourselves, not even suspecting it, have both been gradually raised up to the level where war begins. All our weapons and habits correspond with each other and balance against each other like the beams of a gable. No other women in the world excite less brutality in us, or less desire, than your wives and daughters do; they give us a joy and an anguish of heart which is a sure sign of impending war between us. Doom has transfigured everything here with the colour of storm: your grave buildings shaking with shadow and fire, the neighing horses, figures disappearing into the dark of a colonnade: the future has never impressed me before with such startling clarity. There is nothing to be done. You're already living in the light of the Greek war.

HECTOR. And do the rest of the Greeks think this?

ULYSSES. What they think is no more reassuring. The rest of the Greeks think Troy is wealthy, her warehouses bulging, her soil prolific. They think that they, on the other hand, are living cramped on a rock. And your golden temples and golden wheatfields flashed from your promontories a signal our ships will never forget. It isn't very wise to have such golden gods and vegetables.

HECTOR. This is more like the truth, at last. Greece has chosen Troy for her prey. Then why a declaration of war? It would have been simpler to have taken Troy by surprise when I was away with the army. You would have had her without striking a blow.

ULYSSES. There's a kind of permission for war which can be given only by the world's mood and atmosphere, the feel of its pulse. It would have been madness to undertake a war without that permission. We didn't have it.

HECTOR. But you have it now.

ULYSSES. I think we do.

HECTOR But why against us? Troy is famous for her arts, her justice, her humanity.

ULYSSES. A nation doesn't put itself at odds with its destiny by its crimes, but by its faults. Its army may be strong, its treasury well filled, its poets at the height of inspiration. But one day, why it is no one knows, because of some simple event, such as the citizens wantonly cutting down the trees, or their prince wickedly making off with a woman, or the children getting out of hand, the nation is suddenly lost. Nations, like men, die by imperceptible disorders. We recognize a doomed people by the way they sneeze or pare their nails. There's no doubt you carried off Helen badly.

HECTOR. What fairness of proportion can you see between the rape of one woman, and the possible destruction of a whole people, yours or mine, in war?

ULYSSES. We are speaking of Helen. You and Paris have made a great mistake about Helen. I've known her fifteen years, and watched her carefully. There's no doubt about it: she is one of the rare creatures destiny puts on the earth for its own personal use. They're apparently quite unimportant. It might be not even a person, but a small town, or a village: a little queen, or a child; but if you lay hands on them, watch out! It's very hard to know how to recognize one of these hostages of fate among all the other people and places. You haven't recognized it. You could have laid hands with impunity on our great admirals or one of our kings. Paris could have let himself go with perfect safety in a Spartan bed, or a Theban bed, with generous returns twenty times over; but he chose the shallowest brain, the hardest heart, the narrowest understanding of sex. And so you are lost.

HECTOR. We are giving Helen back to you.

ULYSSES. The insult to destiny can't be taken back.

HECTOR. What are we discussing, then? I'm beginning to see what is really behind your words. Admit it. You want our wealth! You had Helen carried off to give you an honourable pretext for war! I blush for Greece. She will be responsible and ashamed for the rest of time.

ULYSSES. Responsible and ashamed? Do you think so?
The two words hardly agree. Even if we believed we were
responsible for the war, all our generation would have to do
would be to deny it, and lie, to appease the conscience of
future generations. And we shall lie. We'll make that sacrifice.

HECTOR. Ah, well, the die is cast, Ulysses. On with the war!
The more I hate it, the more I find growing in me an
irresistible need to kill. If you won't help me, it were better
you should leave here.

ULYSSES. Understand me, Hector; you have my help. Don't
ask me to interpret fate. All I have tried to do is to read the
world's hand, in the great lines of desert caravans, the wake
of ships, and the track of migrant birds and wandering
peoples. Give me your hand. There are lines there, too. We
won't search to see if their lesson tells the same story. We'll
suppose that these three little lines at the base of Hector's
hand contradict the waves, the wings, and the furrows. I am
inquisitive by nature, and not easily frightened. I'm quite
willing to join issue with fate. I accept your offer of Helen.
I will take her back to Menelaus. I've more than enough
eloquence to convince a husband of his wife's virtue. I will
even persuade Helen to believe it herself. And I'll leave at
once, to avoid any chance of disturbance. Once back on my
ship perhaps we can take the risk of running war on to the
rocks.

HECTOR. Is this part of Ulysses' cunning, or his greatness?

ULYSSES. In this particular instance, I'm using my cunning
against destiny, not against you. It's my first attempt, so I
deserve some credit for it. I am sincere, Hector. If I wanted
war, I should have asked for a ransom more precious to you
than Helen. I am going now. But I can't shake off the feeling
that the road from here to my ship is a long way.

HECTOR. My guard will escort you.

ULYSSES. As long as the road of a visiting king, when he
knows there has been a threat against his life. Where are the
assassins hiding? We're lucky if it's not in the heavens
themselves. And the distance from here to the corner of the

palace is a long way. A long way, taking this first step. Where is it going to carry me among all these perils? Am I going to slip and kill myself? Will part of the cornice fall down on me? It's all new stonework here; at any moment a stone may be dislodged. But courage. Let us go. (*He takes a first step*)

HECTOR. Thank you, Ulysses.

ULYSSES. The first step is safely over. How many more?

HECTOR. Four hundred and sixty.

ULYSSES. Now the second! You know what made me decide to go, Hector?

HECTOR. Yes. Your noble nature.

ULYSSES. Not precisely. Andromache's eyelashes dance as my wife Penelope's do.

(*Enter* ANDROMACHE *and* CASSANDRA)

HECTOR. Were you there all the time, Andromache?

ANDROMACHE. Let me take your arm. I've no more strength.

HECTOR. Did you hear what we said?

ANDROMACHE. Yes. I am broken.

HECTOR. You see, we needn't despair.

ANDROMACHE. We needn't despair for ourselves, perhaps. But for the world, yes. That man is terrible. All the unhappiness of the world is in me.

HECTOR. A moment or two more, and Ulysses will be on board. You see how fast he is travelling. You can follow his progress from here. There he is, on a level with the fountains. What are you doing?

ANDROMACHE. I haven't the strength any longer to hear any more. I am covering up my ears. I won't take my hands away until we know what our fate is to be.

HECTOR. Find Helen, Cassandra!

(AJAX *enters, more drunk than ever. He sees*
ANDROMACHE. *Her back is towards him*)

CASSANDRA. Ulysses is waiting for you down at the harbour, Ajax. Helen will be brought to you there.

AJAX. Helen! To hell with Helen! This is the one I want to get my arms around.

CASSANDRA. Go away, Ajax. That is Hector's wife.

AJAX. Hector's wife! Bravo! I've always liked my friends' wives, my best friends' wives!

CASSANDRA. Ulysses is already half-way there. Hurry.

AJAX. Don't worry, my dear. She's got her hands over her ears. I can say what I like, she can't hear me. If I touched her, now, if I kissed her, certainly! But words she can't hear, what's the matter with that?

CASSANDRA. Everything is the matter with that. Go away, Ajax!

(AJAX, *while* CASSANDRA *tries to force him away from* ANDROMACHE *and* HECTOR, *slowly raises his javelin*)

AJAX. Do you think so? Then I might as well touch her. Might as well kiss her. But chastely, always chastely, with your best friends' wives! What's the most chaste part of your wife, Hector, her neck? So much for her neck. Her ear has a pretty little look of chastity to me. So much for her ear. I'll tell you what I've always found the chastest thing about a woman ... Let me alone, now; let me alone! She can't even hear when I kiss her ... You're so cursed strong! All right, I'm going, I said I was going. Goodbye.

(*He goes*)

(HECTOR *imperceptibly lowers his javelin. At this moment* DEMOKOS *bursts in*)

DEMOKOS. What's this cowardice? You're giving Helen back? Trojans, to arms! They've betrayed us. Fall in! And your war-song is ready! Listen to your war-song!

HECTOR (*striking him*). Have that for your war-song!

DEMOKOS (*falling*). He has killed me!

HECTOR. The war isn't going to happen, Andromache!

(*He tries to take* ANDROMACHE'S *hands from her ears: she resists, her eyes fixed on* DEMOKOS. *The curtain which had begun to fall is lifted little by little*)

ABNEOS. They have killed Demokos! Who killed Demokos?

DEMOKOS. Who killed me? Ajax! Ajax! Kill him!

ABNEOS. Kill Ajax!

HECTOR. He's lying. I am the man who struck him.

DEMOKOS. No. It was Ajax.

ABNEOS. Ajax has killed Demokos. Catch him! Punish him!

HECTOR. I struck you, Demokos, admit it! Admit it, or I'll put an end to you!

DEMOKOS. No, my dear Hector, my good dear Hector. It was Ajax. Kill Ajax!

CASSANDRA. He is dying, just as he lived, croaking like a frog.

ABNEOS. There. They have taken Ajax. There. They have killed him!

HECTOR (*drawing* ANDROMACHE'S *hands away from her ears*). The war will happen.

(*The Gates of War slowly open, to show* HELEN *kissing* TROILUS)

CASSANDRA. The Trojan poet is dead. And now the Grecian poet will have his word.

THE CURTAIN FINALLY FALLS

APPENDIX

APPENDIX

In the stage version at the Apollo Theatre the following passage was substituted for the dialogue between CASSANDRA, HELEN and PEACE on pages 32 and 33:

HELEN. Cassandra, you can see what I can see. You could have helped him to understand me.

CASSANDRA. He understands you only too clearly. And, besides, I see nothing; I never have seen anything, coloured or not. But I can feel the weight of every person who comes towards me. I know what is in store for them by the sensation of suffering which flows into my veins.

HELEN. In fact, you feel what I can see.

CASSANDRA. What I feel in Hector is a suffering too deep to be suffered. He may yet break the reflection in your mirror, Helen. He may have hands great enough to strangle the tiger as it springs.

HELEN. Do you suppose so?

CASSANDRA. There is always something more than one supposes.